Contents

Richard Doyle. Part of the procession from *An Overland Journey to the Great Exhibition* (Chapman & Hall, 1851).

Introduction

The idea for this exhibition was put forward at the time of the National Book League's four linked displays on the theme of *Word and Image*. By examining in sequence the work of Wyndham Lewis, Michael Ayrton, Mervyn Peake and David Jones, the organisers of that series were attempting to set out the relationship (and sometimes the interdependence) which existed between the verbal and graphic expression of men skilled in both modes.

While it is no part of the present exhibition to demonstrate a qualitative similarity between, say, *The Apes of God* and *The Tale of Peter Rabbit*, they are nonetheless both books where, at some point, the author is attempting to influence the reader by pictures as well as words and where the effect of this influence may be of importance. Indeed, at a purely quantitative level, the number of readers likely to be affected by the latter book is vastly greater than the number who have even heard of, let alone read, the former. If we also accept that the readers of *Peter Rabbit* are likely to be much more impressionable, then a case may perhaps be argued for a more intensive study of picture books for children than of words and images for the mature citizen.

One other quantitative factor may also be introduced here, and that is the sheer weight of numbers that is summoned up by the phrase 'children's picture books'. Even if one excludes those books which have not been written and illustrated by the same person, there is still a formidable body of work that has been created for the child reader (or for the child being read to) and this of course would be further swollen if one were to widen the terms of reference even further and include the whole range of children's imaginative fiction alongside picture books.

In view of the large number of books that are thus called in question, and of the many children who may, in one way or another, be coming up against them, this exhibition has finally taken a rather different direction from that of the *Word and Image* series. Instead of simply examining the techniques of a few selected artists, an attempt is being made to consider some of the principles which underlie both the creation of different types of picture book and their critical assessment.

It is all too easy to shrug off the careful analysis of children's books on the grounds either that they are beneath serious critical attention, or that it makes no difference what the adults think, the children are quite capable of asserting their own tastes – which, like the

Frontispiece: 'How many miles to Babylon?' from Mervyn Peake's *Ride a Cockhorse* (item 77).

truth, will ultimately prevail. Nevertheless, if we accept that these books are capable of influencing a child's response both to other books and to the world around him, and if we recognise that the huge number of children's books at present in print raises for many adults a question of choice, then it may perhaps be worth exploring in more detail one or two aspects of contemporary production. The present exhibition aims to do two things. First within the limitations of a fairly confined space, it is designed to show something of the range of current picture books for children, and second, by juxtaposing selected books it seeks to suggest a critical standpoint for their judgement. For 'picture books' are not a homogeneous group. They are not all simply large books with more acreage devoted to pictures than to text. Rather they are capable of being categorised into much more specific groups, each of which may be attempting something different from the others, and for each of which the purpose needs to be understood before the performance can be assessed. Thus the exhibition is divided into a series of broad sections and within these sections several key books are being shown in order to demonstrate points about the group as a whole.

One of the difficulties which has had to be faced in preparing a purposive display of this kind, is inherent in the nature of the books themselves. Many of the best children's books are dynamic rather than static (a point reverted to several times in the pages ahead) and they cannot therefore be assessed through a single page-opening displayed 'under glass'. These books must be looked at page by page in order fully to discover the responsiveness of the illustrator to the movement of his text, and, very often (especially in books dealing with traditional tales or with similar themes) it is necessary to bring two or three books together for comparison.

In consequence, the exhibition has been arranged with a minimum of formality. Only historic items or those of special value have been given permanent places in the display stands; the rest have been laid out in such a way that they can be handled by visitors and examined on points of detail.

The following catalogue sets out the reasons for the inclusion of many of the books and suggests ways in which they may be compared or contrasted with others. A number of 'key items' in each group have been discussed at what may seem to be tiresome length for an exhibition catalogue, but it is to be hoped that the document and its illustrations may have a value in their own right, dissociated from the display.

If a summary can be made of the position which the catalogue tries to assert then it is perhaps the permanence of traditional values in book illustration. Book illustrators (even when they have written their own texts) are associates in a partnership; they are not there to overwhelm the substance of the book, but to work with it in the most fitting way that they can. Their responsibility is to reflect truly the imaginative tenor of the text (or, in the case of books without text, of the subject) and to create a sequence or group of pictures which add up to a consistent whole. It is a recognition of this fact that lies behind the greatness of the English school of book illustration (and in children's books this includes such names as Blake and Mulready, Cruikshank and Lear, Doyle

and Caldecott) and the present exhibition seeks to show that the tradition is not only still to be respected but can be abandoned only at the peril of vacuity or pretentiousness.

Among the virtues of the traditional approach to book illustration is its care for the details of a picture's narrative content and design. This is not to say that there is always necessarily something going on in the illustrations, but that there is nearly always a nuance of detail for the eye to feed upon and one which in the best work will be in complete harmony (and may even be visually integrated) with the printed text.

Too often at present we are finding artists lured from the traditional style of book illustration by the graphic possibilities of modern colour printing processes or by the requirements of international syndication – the one leading, as often as not, to a display of the painter's skill or lack of it, the other to triteness. While the present over-production of picture books continues it is doubtful if anything can be done about it, but the necessarily limited 'historical' sections in the exhibition have been prepared in part to show that our own time has no monopoly in either commercial enterprise, technical accomplishment or artistic genius. If Maurice Sendak is the hero of this exhibition it is because (as he himself would be the first to recognise) he has the history of illustration in his bones.

The organiser of the exhibition makes no apology that neither his selection of books nor his remarks in the catalogue have been primarily made for the benefit of children. Naturally he hopes that children will attend the exhibition and enjoy many of the books that are on display (at least they will be able to look at them or read them from cover to cover, which is more than happens at many like exhibitions). He will also not be unduly surprised if young visitors show a perverse liking for certain books which have been criticised in the following pages. It is the adults who control children's lives who have too often decided that there are no alternatives to such books, and it is for such adults that this experiment in practical criticism is intended.

B.A.

Richard Doyle. A vignette from *A Journal . . . Kept in the Year 1840* (Smith, Elder, 1885).

Bibliographic Information

The form of entry for all the contemporary books discussed in the catalogue aims to give the following basic information:

Title as given on the title page;

Author (and illustrator, where there is a distinction), usually employing the conventional terms 'by' or 'illustrated by', but sometimes adopting a different form of words as given on the title page;

Publisher of the edition shown in the exhibition;

Date of the first English edition of the book shown in the exhibition (but an attempt has also been made to give both the publisher and the first edition date of all books which received prior publication in the United States of America. Only occasionally however has it been possible to note either the American editions of books first published in Great Britain, or the original publication details of books first published in foreign languages. It is recognized that this might have been helpful, but without more reliable information supplied by publishers in their imprints it has proved too time-consuming to do consistently);

Price at the date of going to press, included here in order to give at least a rough indication of the varying claims of some books to be considered for the 'popular' market or for those buyers, chiefly librarians, who are willing to spend more substantial sums of money. The catalogue is not primarily a buying-list however, and paperback editions of the picture books under discussion have only been noted where they help to emphasise a critical detail. While, naturally enough, a welcome has been given to the appearance of many picture books in cheap paperback editions, it ought to be noted that the resultant reduction in size, or lengthening of print-run (or both factors combined) produce a book which is not often comparable to the hardback original.

For the historical entries a standard short-title catalogue entry has been adopted based upon either the book's title page or its cover-title. No profound research has been undertaken into the dating of undated items and the conjectural dates supplied in brackets are usually based either on the catalogue at the Victoria and Albert Museum Library, or on published catalogues, such as the Toronto Public Library's *Osborne Collection of Early Children's Books* (Bibliography item 18), or on internal evidence. Wherever it has been thought necessary to include further specific facts about the books' preparation, illustration or method of production this has usually been included in the annotation.

Acknowledgements

Many people have helped me in the preparation of this exhibition, whose founders must really be seen as Mrs Nancy Chambers and Mrs Valerie Alderson, who allowed me to develop my ideas about picture books in the review columns respectively of *Children's Book News* and *Children's Book Review*, and Miss Eleanor von Schweinitz who taught me (and continues to teach me) to 'look at picture books' and who, properly, should have written this catalogue. From her pen much that is here diffuse or hesitant would have been precise and authoritative.

As work has progressed I have been greatly helped by Miss Marilyn Edwards, the Children's Book Officer of the NBL, who has curbed some of my more wayward pronouncements ; by Miss Irene Whalley and Miss Ann Hobbs of the Victoria and Albert Museum Library, who have been most courteous in allowing me to use the marvellous resources of the Guy Little and the Renier collections ; by Miss Janet Holman of the Inner London Education Authority's Media Resources Centre ; by Mr. Duncan Skinner of Bocardo Press whose patience during proofing and printing of this catalogue has been of superhuman dimensions ; and by Mr Michael Pountney of W. H. Smith & Sons, who holds such enlightened views about the value of Walt Disney Productions *et hoc genus omne*.

Above all however my gratitude must go to Miss Caroline Dingwall, the Publications Officer of the NBL, who has devoted more time and more care than I deserve to the preparation of this catalogue. But for her watchful attention at all stages of its compilation, her helpful advice, and her arduous work in typing my ugly manuscript and preparing it for the printers, it is difficult to see how visitors to the exhibition would have received anything but the most rudimentary of guides. To her also has fallen the laborious task of compiling the index. Needless to say, all responsibility for errors and omissions rests with myself.

Finally, I must emphasize categorically that the plan of this catalogue and the opinions expressed in it are mine alone and must in no way be attributed to the NBL, who have been so hospitable as to house the exhibition and to allow me full freedom in directing it to critical rather than descriptive ends.

The National Book League would like to thank the Victoria and Albert Museum for the kind loan of books from their Library ; and the Trustees of the Linder Collection of the Works of Beatrix Potter for permission to display a number of items.

1. AT FIRST SIGHT

For many children the first experience of looking into books may be of the most elementary kind : seeing a random series of pictures, usually of what are thought to be 'everyday objects', very often unaccompanied by any text at all. Indeed the quality 'book' resides only in the mechanism of the hinges fastening together a series of unrelated pictures and, although both the producers of such books and many of the parents who buy them may see in them useful points of departure for the naming of objects or for conversation with the child, there may nonetheless be a conflict of interests. How far, at this early stage, is the child physically capable of distinguishing lines and shapes on the page, and then how capable of relating them to objects in the world of experience ? Is it not axiomatic that the design of the book should aim at a clear, uncomplicated representationalism and its content lean rather towards the domestic than the natural or exotic ? The time has passed when rural pursuits were the focus of every child's attention and books of farm animals may now be seen as something which many children will understand and appreciate at a later stage than books of everyday things.

At this early stage of development the child is inexperienced at interpreting pictures and it is important that the objects pictured should, on the one hand correspond fairly closely in appearance to their real counterparts, and, on the other hand be printed plainly without too much distracting detail or confusion of colour. Even so, young children will often regard their first books as something more akin to a primitive flail or a novel kind of building brick ; for which reason there is a tendency for these first picture books to be made of rag or board – materials which may be proof against heavy handling and chewing, but which call for special care in printing and manufacture.

(1) **My Favourite Toys** *Sandle's*, n.d. 12p.
An anonymous board book, typical of those which have been produced for many years for mass-retailing through confectioners, sub-post-offices and toyshops.

(2) **Farm Friends** *Bancroft*, n.d. 25p.
An anonymous rag book of the same kind. The blurred printing (suggestive of long print-runs) and the muddled composition do not make it easy for the child to identify the animals. Washing instructions are included.

(3) **A Ladybird First Picture Book** by Ethel and Harry Wingfield *Ladybird* 1970 15p.
(4) **First Things**: a child's world of familiar objects. Photographed in colour by Thomas Matthiesen *Collins* 1967 50p.
Two object books whose introductory notes indicate their common purpose and whose randomly selected pictures coincide with surprising frequency. The realistic paintings of the *First Picture Book* are, like the photographs of *First Things*, concerned only with clarity of representation and there is little to choose between the exactness of their renderings (although the Wingfields' orange has just that much more hint of the essential messiness of oranges than the rather suave photograph by Mr Matthiesen).

(5) **Animal Babies** by Robert Broomfield *Bodley Head* 1973, 35p.
In an attempt to overcome the mundane conventions of these simple books, some publishers have encouraged established picture-book artists to design examples which have a more modern appearance. *Animal Babies* is perhaps the most attractive of four 'Bodley Head Board Books', and it contrasts sharply with the foregoing items. Even so, Robert Broomfield has not been entirely successful in distinguishing the animals against their backgrounds. It is unlikely that small, board-book-chewing children will have sufficiently developed visual experience fully to apprehend the nature of Mr Broomfield's rabbit and kitten.

(6) **Indoors** by Maureen Roffey *Bodley Head* 1973, 35p.
A recognition of the limitations that are imposed upon the modern artist is evident in another of the 'Bodley Head Board Books'. For the 1973 edition of *Indoors* Miss Roffey changed the 1968 pictures of a sewing machine and a mincing machine – both far too stylised for a young child to understand – and replaced them with a jelly and a toothbrush. Even so, the huge difference in scale between the toothbrush and the facing telephone are decidedly disconcerting. (See page 11).

Comparisons from the Past

(7) **Child's Picture Book** (Cover title). *Harvey & Darton*. n.d. [c.1840]
Four little books of hand-coloured pictures, bound in one volume. The intention was specifically to provide something to look at which 'may perhaps . . . instruct as well as amuse us' and so tenuous is the link between text and picture that it is clear that the books were devised and sold on the strength of their visual appeal.

(8) **The Panoramic Alphabet of Trades** *Darton & Co*. n.d. [c.1850]
A popular alphabet book printed on linen and rather hastily coloured by hand.

(9) **Little Pets** by Tony Brice. *Collins* Board Books 1945. (NY, *Rand McNally* n.d.).

2. ALPHABET BOOKS

A natural extension of the 'object' picture-book takes in the territory of the abc, where a like randomness of picture-sequence may prevail but where there is the superficial ordering principle of the twenty-six letters of the alphabet. While it is true that many alphabets in books of the past were intended as a foundation for the teaching of reading (see items 162 and 164) the most notable work being done today is in the spirit of Walter Crane rather than Dr Mavor – the artists often bearing in mind the need for clear typography but not allowing didactic regulations to interfere with fancy in the choice of subject for their twenty-six pictures. It would be a mistake therefore to judge all alphabet books as either 'learning books' or very simple picture-books and some of the examples that here follow have clearly been designed primarily to challenge the child's powers of perception, his imagination, his sense of humour. They may do this not simply through the medium of their illustrations but also through the selection and juxtaposition of their chosen words. The pleasure that young children gain from mouthing such syllables as 'iguana' or 'violin – volcano – vulture' far outweighs the smooth ease of 'ink' or 'van', whose simplicity attracts the less imaginative compiler of abc's.

The scope for analysing the permutations in the various artists' choice of subjects to fit their twenty-six letters is enormous. ('A for Apple' is a tradition that dies hard; what a procession of Queens appears for 'Q'; what subterfuges are employed to cope with 'X'). Comparisons in the notes however have been confined to making specific points related to illustrative styles and no attempt has been made consistently to assess the suitability of the subjects chosen or the value which the books may have for anyone trying strictly 'to teach the alphabet' through them.

(10) **b is for bear** by Dick Bruna *Methuen* 1967, 80p.
A book whose presentation of objects in a stylised, two-dimensional pattern carries forward a feature found in many object-recognition books. The use of strong outlines and flat patches of colour was not invented by Dick Bruna but it is a style which he has made very much his own. It tends to be more successful with simple objects like apples and keys than with more problematic ones like eskimoes and yellow yawners. In 1971, *b is for bear* was converted into an abc frieze, possibly under the influence of:

(11) **The ABC Frieze** by Michael Spink *Cape* 1968, 65p.
which may in turn owe something to the influence of Bruna's simple patterns. Certainly the bolder, simpler drawings are best — the ones that try to be clever ('Jockey', 'Queen', 'Viking') end up by being confusing. 'Exit' is not really a good way out for 'X'.

(12) **My Own ABC** *Sandle's*, n.d. 30p.
A popular board book whose pictures are as sterile as its adaptation of the traditional verses on which it is based.

(13) Celestino Piatti's **Animal ABC** *Benn* 1965, £1·25.
Piatti's characteristic use of heavy, brushed outlines gives a certain monumental quality to his animals which suits the Rhinoceros and the Elephant but leads to some confusion with Chameleon, Frog and Quetzal. The Xopiatti is a neat solution for 'X', but the vanished Jaguar who has walked off the page is a cheat.

(14) **ABC with People** by Jonathan Milne *Macmillan* 1971, £1·05.
Like Piatti, Milne is simple in a way that demands a fairly sophisticated response. His fashionable, two-dimensional colour work, his reliance upon the humour of sketched attitudes and expressions, produce pictures more closely related to advertisement design than children's book illustration. Compare for instance his clown and his queen with those of John Burningham (16) where there may be a similar dependence upon 'flat' painting, but where the greater richness of colour and detail, and the broader sense of humour make a far more lively appeal. According to the imprint, the book originated in Australia.

(15) **ABC** by Brian Wildsmith *Oxford University Press* 1962, 90p.
The publication of this *ABC* in 1962 stands out as something of a landmark in the history of contemporary picture books. The bold use of colour — not only in the paintings but also on the page surfaces — and the superlative lithography of the Brüder Rosenbaum, were the crucial influences in what became a vogue for hectic chromaticism. The delicate adjustments of line and colour native to the best book illustration tended to become swamped by ubiquitous purples and carmines and critical judgement was swayed

by virtuoso and not-so-virtuoso printing techniques. This *ABC* however is above the battle. Its careful management of the printed words is a reflection of the vision and control that went into its sequence of paintings, each one of which gives a vibrancy to its subject rarely seen before in any children's book.

(16) John Burningham's **ABC** *Cape* 1964, £1·05.
Published two years after Brian Wildsmith's *ABC*, this volume shows its influence, especially in the use of textured colour pages as a background to the white lettering. But in every respect the book is the artist's own, with his particular sense of pattern and his very individual wit. Eight of the subjects chosen by John Burningham coincide with those chosen by Brian Wildsmith, but one has only to compare Iguana for Iguana, Queen for Queen, to appreciate the radical difference between the two approaches. In Mr Burningham's book, the smile of the first and the caricatured pomp of the second are touches which set up responses evoked by 'illustration' rather than by 'painting'.

(17) Helen Oxenbury's **ABC of Things** *Heinemann* 1971, £1·00.
It is difficult to avoid seeing similarities between the work of John Burningham and his wife Helen Oxenbury, but quite unjustifiable to suggest anything more than a general climatic reason. Their outstanding command of design and colour, their ready pictorial wit are in fact very distinct (compare the umbrellas and the xylophones) and the humour in John Burningham's *ABC* is in his wife's alphabet book made decidedly more explicit, with the bunching of words and objects offering a variety of possibilities for 'situation comedy'. (See page 11).

(18) **The Alphabet Book** by Rodney Peppé *Longman Young Books* 1968, £1·10.
Altogether less original in its flat, cheerful graphics, but with an unusual linking of letters through the short texts of each page opening. 'Elephant', who also occurs with other characters in the final 'Z for Zoo', is particularly successful.

(19) **Annie, Bridget and Charlie** an ABC for children of rhymes recollected by Jessie G. Townsend, illustrated by Jan Pienkowski *Cape* 1967, £1·05.
As a piece of self-conscious book design *Annie, Bridget and Charlie* shows up the lack of style and professional application in books of similar intention, such as *ABC with People* (14). Nevertheless, there is a lifelessness at the heart of this picture book which is by no means wholly attributable to the weak limericks that make up its text. For all the thought that has gone into the juxtaposition of colours, the planning of pages and the toying with decorative frames, the pictures are finally just beautifully composed patterns, more fit for the showrooms of Habitat than the child's own bookcase.

(20) **The First ABC** devised by Frank Waters, and pictures drawn by Charles Mozley *Watts* 1970, 60p.
In no sense a 'first alphabet' when compared with the simple graphic work and page-layouts of, say, Dick Bruna (10) or John Burningham (16). Although the upper and lower case letters are boldly placed, (except for the nervous cramming of 'XYZ'), the rest of the page-openings tend to confusion. Many of the paintings are blurred in their details and the size ratios of the grouped drawings (eg:

Item 3

Item 4

Item 6

First things. A comparison of the treatment of similar subjects in a photograph and a picture (above); and of the changed page opening for the 1968 and 1973 editions of *Indoors* (below).

Item 17

Item 10

Item 16

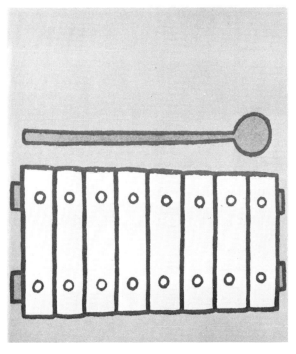

ABC's. Three pictures of 'X for Xylophone'.

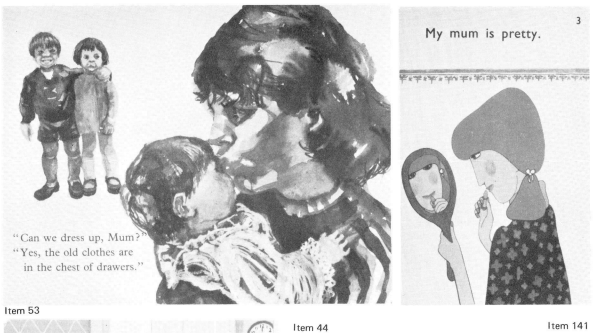

"Can we dress up, Mum?"
"Yes, the old clothes are
    in the chest of drawers."

My mum is pretty.

Item 53

Item 44

Item 141

Item 43

A collection of mums. Four different portrayals of the mother-figure taken from
books in the sections 'About the house' and 'At the point of reading'.

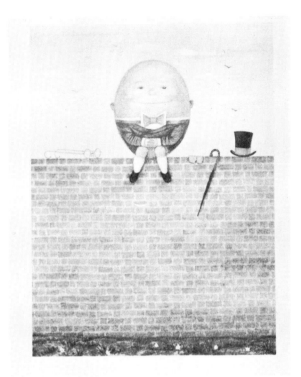

HUMPTY DUMPTY
Humpty Dumpty sat on a wall,
Humpty Dumpty had a great fall;
All the King's horses and all the King's men
Couldn't put Humpty together again.

110

↑ Item 72   ↓ Item 71   ↑ Item 75   ↓ Item 66

Come, let's to bed,
    Says Sleepy-head;
Tarry a while, says Slow;
    Put on the pan,
Says Greedy Nan,
    Let's sup before we go.

72

Come let's to bed

"Come let's to bed," says Sleepy Head,
"Tarry awhile," says Slow.
"Put on the pan," says Greedy Nan,
"We'll sup before we go."

Nursery rhymes (1). Raymond Brigg's changed view of Humpty Dumpty in books published in 1962 and 1966 (above); and a contrast between a true and false sense of tradition in the work of Harold Jones and Hilda Boswell (below).

Humpty Dumpty sat on a wall,
Humpty Dumpty had a great fall.
All the king's horses and all the king's men
Couldn't put Humpty Dumpty together again.

3

IF ALL THE WORLD

If all the world was paper,
    And all the sea was ink,
If all the trees were bread and cheese,
    What should we have to drink?

99

↑ Item 76   ↓ Item 67   ↑ Item 75   ↓ Item 77

LITTLE Tommy Tucker
Sings for his supper,
What shall we give him?
White bread and butter.
How shall he cut it
Without e're a knife?
How shall he marry
Without e're a wife?

Nursery rhymes (2). Four examples of the presence of the artist in nursery rhyme books: Brian Wildsmith's stolid page (yet another Humpty Dumpty), Raymond Briggs's use of collage, the Johnstones' 'modernism', and the imaginative vision of Mervyn Peake.

'thistle', 'tree') are hardly within the comprehension of 'first' readers. As to the carving up of Edward Lear's nonsense alphabets (not 'limericks', *pace* Mr Waters, page 2), the less said about this the better. The original texts may be seen in:

(21) **The Complete Nonsense of Edward Lear** edited by Holbrook Jackson *Faber* 1947, £1·90 alongside.

(22) **ABC** penned and illustrated by Edward Lear himself *Longman Young Books* 1965 (NY, 1965).
First publication of a manuscript alphabet by Edward Lear, which gives a juster impression of the balance between text and drawing on the page demanded by the artist but lacking in the reprinted alphabets in *Complete Nonsense* (above). A printed version of the Ms. text is given at the end of the book.

(23) **A Apple Pie** by Kate Greenaway *Warne*. First published by *George Routledge* in 1886. 85p.
There is reason to suggest that this historic picture book is ceasing to be regarded simply as quaint or mustily old-fashioned and is once again coming to have a direct appeal to children. The composition of the large pages and the expressiveness of attitude in the child groups (to say nothing of the pie!) have an immediacy of attraction far removed from static patterning of ostensibly 'simpler' books, such as those by Celestino Piatti (13) and Jonathan Milne (14). For all the mechanical aids to modern printing, however, we do not seem to be able to match the delicate line and colour effects achieved by Edmund Evans in his first printing from wood-blocks, done in series, colour by colour. The same too might be said of the recent publication of:

(24) **Kate Greenaway's Alphabet.** A facsimile of the 1885 edition. *Cape* 1973, 50p.
See items 31 and 32, and accompanying note.

(25) **Illustrated Comic Alphabet** by Amelia Frances Howard-Gibbon. *Oxford University Press* 1967, £1·00. (*Toronto Public Library* 1966).
Another example of an ABC reproduced from a Victorian manuscript (1859) – thought to be the earliest Canadian picture book. It bears witness to the ease with which the nineteenth century artist could come to terms with his child audience in primarily narrative pictures.

Comparisons from the Past

(26) **A New Lottery Book of Birds and Beasts,** for children to learn their letters as soon as they can speak. Newcastle, printed by T. Saint for W. Charnley, 1771.
An early pictorial alphabet book, notable as one of the first books to be illustrated by the wood-engraver Thomas Bewick. His later work, which refined the technique of 'white-line engraving', was to cause a revolution in the appearance of pictures in many children's books.

(27) **The Picture Alphabet** for the instruction and amusement of boys and girls by 'H. S'. Otley, printed by William Walker, 1830.
A cheap alphabet, using a variety of ornamented and ultra-bold letters along with its woodcut illustrations.

(28) **Aunt Busy Bee's Alphabet of Nouns:** or, good child's ABC. *Dean & Son.* n.d. [1852].
In Dean's series of 'original and superior six-penny books'. Like item 8 above, a popular mid-nineteenth century ABC.

(29) **The Farm-Yard Alphabet.** *George Routledge & Sons.* n.d. [c.1880].
A simple alphabet for the young child, printed by Edmund Evans. The large letter-pictures are interspersed with a miscellany of monochrome illustrations which were probably taken from stock blocks.

(30) **The Alphabet of Old Friends** *George Routledge & Sons* n.d. [1875] (Walter Crane's Toy Books, shilling series).
A sumptuously decorated book, drawing its subjects from nursery rhyme themes.

(31) **A Apple Pie** by Kate Greenaway. *George Routledge & Sons*, 1886.
(32) **Kate Greenaway's Alphabet.** *George Routledge & Sons*, 1885.
Early printings of the books shown at 23 and 24, and included here so that the quality of colour-printing may be compared. *Kate Greenaway's Alphabet* was itself a coloured version of some line drawings which the artist had done for her edition of Mavor's *English Spelling Book*, 1885 (see item 163). Observations by Edmund Evans himself on his colour printing methods and on his association with children's book illustrators of the day may be found in his *Reminiscences* (Bibliography item 37) pages 32–4 and 55–65.

3. COUNTING BOOKS

At first the connection between 'abc' books and '123' books may be thought a close one. The following notes however attempt to distinguish ways in which number sequences offer greater scope to the compilers and illustrators of counting books so that their style may merge with that of the simple story book (See Section 7) or the traditional cumulative rhyme or tale.

(33) **The First Counting Book** by Margaret Durden *Watts* 1970, 60p.
(34) **Numbers** by M. E. Gagg, illustrated by G. Robinson *Ladybird* 1959, 15p.
Two examples of counting books in the workaday style of the popular coloured picture book. The brightness of the page openings however serves chiefly to distract the eye from the poor draughtsmanship and the lack of imagination in the choice and arrangement of subjects. However serviceable for teaching numbers, the books teach the eye nothing.

(35) **123** by Brian Wildsmith *Oxford University Press* 1965, £1·10.
In sharpest contrast to the above, Brian Wildsmith shows here virtuosity in the organisation and colouring of shapes on pages and in the progressive development of shapes throughout the book. He has himself stated on a number of occasions that the basic, mathematical intention of a counting book stimulated him to design a volume where abstraction would predominate and one of the exciting features of *123* is the way in which the designs and the rudimentary object patterns can stimulate imaginative responses and discussion among young children. The

possibilities, for instance, in his treatment of the numbers 3 and 4 ('the tumbling boxes') stirs the child's sense in a way impossible with Margaret Durden's three rabbits and four boats, and the use of mosaic patterning with in the shapes gives liveliness to what might otherwise be a too static composition and creates a visual metaphor for infinity.

(36) **Numbers of Things** by Helen Oxenbury *Heinemann* 1967, 90p.
While there is a 'design' element here which affords comparison with the work of Jan Pienkowski in *Annie, Bridget and Charlie* (19), this book is saved from being mere decoration by the personality of its inhabitants. Compare '3 children' with those on the title page of *Annie*, and compare, where possible, the animals (eg : '5 cats' and the cat at 'N for Nat'). There is a sublime idiocy about Miss Oxenbury's creatures which is at once more comical and more heart-warming.

(37) **Finding 1 to 10** by George Adamson *Faber* 1968, 90p.
A clever idea which has foundered by being too cleverly carried out. In a playbook like *Where is the Green Parrot ?* (169) the child's pleasure in searching the picture stems from his growing confidence in his own accomplishment. Here the searching demands almost adult abilities – not simply to descry the objects in the highly confused graphic composition, but also to recognise the nature of the objects themselves ('love-in-a-mist' ?, 'graduates' ?, 'news reporters' ?).

Just as alphabet books like those by Rodney Peppé (18) and Kate Greenaway (23) seek to impose some continuity of interest throughout the twenty-six letters, so the cumulative principle inherent in counting books can be used to produce a unified sequence from cover to cover. This may be simple, as with such books as :

(38) **123 to the Zoo** by Eric Carle *Hamish Hamilton* 1969, £1·25. (NY, *World*, 1968) ; and
(39) **Teddybears 1 to 10** by Susanna Gretz *Benn* 1969, 75p.
In each of these instances the illustrator captures and holds attention through continuity. Mr Carle's train gradually assembling itself, arriving and emptying at the zoo is neatly devised, although the use of cut tissue paper to make the pictures gives a crudity to the design which is confusing, and which is not fully overcome by the gay colouring. Susanna Gretz's splendidly gormless bears, however, have an elegance of finish which sacrifices neither colour nor simplicity. They exert the automatic appeal of their kind and their progress from punch-drunk dilapidation to cleansed self-satisfaction makes a small, completely pictorial story.

Further developments are also possible. In the following three examples the idea of number is conveyed primarily through events, although, in the first two, some prominence is given to printed figures.

(40) **Jeanne-Marie Counts her Sheep** by Françoise *Brockhampton* 1955, £1·05. (NY, *Scribner* 1957). Part of a series of picture books about Jeanne-Marie, all characterised by Françoise's illustrations in the rustic style.

The repetition of numbers is insistent enough, but the presence of Patapon among the accumulating lambs frustrates object-counting.

(41) **Sixes and Sevens** by John Yeoman, illustrated by Quentin Blake *Blackie* 1971, £1·10.
An altogether more complex cumulative story, both in its verbal style and in the way that each fresh group of passengers on the raft is linked back to the previous group. The illustrations are correspondingly more intricate, but always full of humour – especially as the raft's cargo increases and anarchy draws ever nearer.

(42) **Six Foolish Fishermen** by Benjamin Elkin *Brockhampton* 1958, £1·05. (Wis. *Hale* 1957).
A traditional joke, which makes excellent use of vignetted illustrations on each page-opening while it puts across the foolishness of the innumerate fishermen. One of the indirect advantages of the joke is that it may convince the youthful mathematician of how much cleverer he is than the book's participants.

4. ABOUT THE HOUSE

In the transition from books which mostly consist of unrelated pictures to picture story-books proper, there is a small group of books which concentrate on the routines of domestic life. They introduce the child to the idea of narrative sequence by presenting him with a linked series of events which might form part of his own experience of the day at home. They show well-known objects or situations, which are usually accompanied by a simple descriptive text, and, more than any other group of books in this exhibition, they call forth reticent, unpretentious and often designedly amateurish illustrations. Their intention is utilitarian rather than aesthetic and they have no crying need for too luxurious a graphic style. Nevertheless there is scope within these limits for a wide variety of illustrative approaches and a mundane purpose is still no excuse for derivative or lifeless pictorialism.

These books also raise at its most immediate the question of an author's or artist's assumptions about his subject, the norm of family life portrayed tending very much towards an average gentility. When this is carried through with the naturalness of *Wheels* (47) or the rough and tumble absorption of *Lucy and Tom's Day* (51) it is of no account, but in books of lesser artistic standing – and most of the books about domestic affairs are just that – it provides a further ingredient in a generally torpid mixture.

(43) **Papa Small** by Lois Lenski *Oxford University Press* 1957, 45p.
First published in America in 1951, *Papa Small* is a prototype of the genre. It is hard to account for the popularity of this moon-faced family, going about their daily and weekly routines, except by admitting the appeal to children of the elementary graphic style and their pleasure in seeing another family at its chores. (It will be all too easy to account for the book's probable damnation by the Daughters of Feminine Liberation. The domestic roles of Mr and Mrs Small confirm all that is deemed worst in the traditional repression of Mama).

(44) **Shopping with Mother** by M. E. Gagg, illustrated by J. H. Wingfield *Ladybird* 1958, 15p.
For all their mooniness the Small Family at least had graphic character and an air of engaged activity – qualities decidedly lacking in the orderly but lifeless portrayal of this family occupation.

(45) **Tim's Family Goes Down the High Street** by Pat Albeck *Nelson* 1970, 60p.
In the matter of text there is not much to choose between this book, with its leaden phrasing, and the descriptiveness of the previous item. An attempt has been made, however, to give it a more 'modern' appearance by the modish two-dimensional draughtsmanship and the flat patterning of the (not very exciting) colours. The result avoids the immediately comprehensible pseudo-realism of the Ladybird book but replaces it with no compensatory graphic verve.

(46) **Joe and the Nursery School** by Alison Prince and Joan Hickson *BBC* with *Methuen Children's Books* 1972, 75p.
A similarly 'modern' but dead approach, transferring into a picture-book graphic designs planned for television. Certainly Joe is a more attractive character than Tim in the previous item, and the colouring, for all its hotness, is more appealing, but the flat design symbolises the book's lack of vitality and its abstraction from the situation it purports to describe.

(47) **Wheels** by Katharine Hoskyns and Jenny Joseph *Longman Young Books* 1966, 30p.
Bearing in mind the unpretentious aims of many of these simple books, the series to which *Wheels* belongs offers a more natural and satisfying combination of text and picture than many of its more trendy competitors. There is character and a sense of warmth in the text and, while the pictures are simple to the point of crudity, they nevertheless reflect well the progress of the story and make clever use of the page shape. (In this volume there is a subdued but neatly managed series of pictorial references to the idea of 'Wheels' which makes the chief subject of the book).

(48) **Boots** also by Katharine Hoskyns and Jenny Joseph *Longman Young Books* 1966, 30p.
is entertaining in a similar way.

(49) **The Toolbox** by Anne and Harlow Rockwell *Hamish Hamilton* 1971, £1·30. (NY, *Macmillan* 1971).
A book which borders on the object-recognition books of Section 1, above, but which wins a place here by virtue of its carefully planned text sequence and because it is an example of a skilled graphic artist turning his talent to simple descriptive work. The drawing of the objects, their colouring, the way that they are placed on the page is exemplary and leads the child not only into a discussion of 'the toolbox' but also into an apprehension of the tools themselves.

A measure of the book's success can be gauged by comparing *The Toolbox* with its successor :

(50) **Machines** by Anne and Harlow Rockwell *Hamish Hamilton* 1973, £1·10. (NY, *Macmillan*, 1972).
where the intentionally simple text and pictures cannot cope either with explanations ('block and tackle', 'gear') or with the wide range of subjects that are introduced.

(51) **Lucy and Tom's Day** written and drawn by Shirley Hughes *Gollancz* 1960, 60p.
A picture book whose individuality lifts it above most of the standardised series productions so prevalent in this category and gives some sense of the *actuality* of children at home. *Lucy and Tom's Day* was Shirley Hughes's first picture book and it typifies her distinctive handling of tousled children in the jumble of family life. At times since the book appeared in 1960, Miss Hughes has seemed to be parodying herself but in such successors as :

(52) **The Trouble with Jack** by Shirley Hughes *Bodley Head* 1970, 65p,
she captures most perceptively the nuances of child gesture and behaviour.

(53) **Let's Play Mums and Dads** by Renate Meyer *Bodley Head* 1970, £1·05.
A portrayal of the grubby reality of children's games more intense than that of Shirley Hughes. Moreover by passing up the predictable possibilities of 'dressing up' as a picture book theme (see next item), Renate Meyer directs attention to the child's absorption in his make-believe world. The subtlety with which the weight and colour of the pictures is used to distinguish the change in mood of the story reinforces the sense that this is a picture book that studies children rather than one which will directly engage their attention. (For further notes on the critical issues raised by Renate Meyer's work, see items 198 and 346).

(54) **Dressing Up** by David Mackay, Brian Thompson and Pamela Schaub. Illustrated by Edward McLachlan *Penguin:* a Breakthrough Reading Book 1973, 12p. (*Longman* 1970).
A treatment of the same theme which neglects imaginative involvement in the interests of mere description. The illustrations appear to be heavily influenced by the style of Tomi Ungerer (see item 272 ff).

(55) **In the Busy Town** by Ali Migutsch *Collins* 1972, 75p. (Ravensburg, *Otto Maier* 1971).
A mildly amusing, but rather obvious, exercise for the child's roving eye, derived from but without the pervasive energy of :

(56) **What Do People Do all Day ?** by Richard Scarry *Collins* 1968, £1·25. (NY, *Random House* 1968).
While the story element in the text descends to the cosy from time to time, its factual content is usually sufficient to support the engrossing detail of the pictures and their accompanying captions. Such scenes as the building of a house, the voyaging ship and the sawmill have all the fascination of a working drawing, enhanced for children by the antics of the Busytown population, who dispose of any latent didacticism with the same briskness with which Sergeant Murphy accounts for Gorilla Bananas.

Comparisons from the Past

(57) **The Toy Primer** in **The Pet Lamb Picture Book** *George Routledge & Sons*. n.d. [1873]
With the nouns listed at the head of the text, this was clearly also intended to be used as an early reading book. The colour printing is by Kronheim.

(58) **At Home** Illustrated by J. G. Sowerby. Decorated by Thomas Crane. *Marcus Ward & Co.* n.d. [1881].
High-Victorian living displayed in high-Victorian graphic style, the text built in to pages of elaborately worked pictures and borders.

(59) **The 'Little Folks' Picture Gallery** *Cassell, Petter & Galpin.* n.d. [c.1875].
Domestic scenes engraved on wood and first used in *Little Folks* magazine. Their binding up here represents an economical use of capital resources.

(60) **Under Mother's Wing** Illustrated by J. (ie : I) K(leinmichel). *Wells, Gardner, Darton & Co.* n.d. [?1900].
(61) **Bunte Bilder. Images Jolies. Gay Images**
Esslingen, *J. T. Schreiber.* n.d.
Two examples of internationalism in the picture-book market of the nineteenth century. Both stem very much from the German tradition of 'the family book', which itself owes a debt to that very early picture book, devised at once to teach simple facts about the everyday world and to inculcate a Latin vocabulary :
(62) **Orbis Sensualium Pictus** by Johann Amos Comenius. Facsimile of the first English edition translated by Charles Hoole in 1659, and illustrated with copper engraving. *Oxford University Press* 1968 (The Juvenile Library.)

(63) **Neuester Orbis Pictus** oder die Welt in Bildern für fromme Kinder. Facsimile of the German edition of 1838. *Insel Verlag,* 1970.
A late German adaptation of the Comenian principle.

(64) **Ett Hem** en bilderbok av Carl Larsson, Stockholm, *Bonniers* 1968.
Facsimile with modern text of a famous Swedish book first published in 1904. The huge paintings, originally printed without facing text, portray family scenes 'at home'.

5. A COMPENDIUM

(65) **The Nutshell Library** by Maurice Sendak.
Comprising *Alligators all Around; Chicken Soup with Rice; One Was Johnny;* and *Pierre. Collins* 1964, 80p. (NY, *Harper* 1962). Produced in separate volumes, *Collins* 1968, 50p each.

Since this 'library' contains an alphabet book, a counting book, a book of months and a cautionary tale, it is in fair way to being the child's Compleat Companion into literacy. And such is the humour and warmth of its accomplishment that one could wish the child little else were he to be stranded on the proverbial desert island. The attractiveness of Sendak's beautifully rounded texts and of his muted, but very expressive, drawings is enhanced by the littleness of the books and the compactness of their decorated box, now of much inferior construction compared with earlier editions. How strange therefore that (largely at the behest of public librarians) an edition of these four books should have been published in a format some three and a half times larger than the original. Gone are the neatness, the decorated box and the exact balancing of line, colour and decoration on the pages.

6. THE PICTURE OF NURSERY RHYMES

At the same time as the child is meeting the simple picture-books so far discussed, he may also find himself introduced to the pleasure of nursery rhymes. Unlike the catalogues of object and event in the alphabet book and domestic tale however, the nursery rhyme book can exist independent of any illustration without losing its essential quality (as can be seen in the recent reissue by the Bodley Head of James Orchard Halliwell's *The Nursery Rhymes of England*, with its few, spare decorations by Maureen Roffey). A lyric like 'I had a little nut-tree', a jingle like 'Hey diddle diddle' or a piece of satisfying nonsense like 'The man of Newington' needs no supplement by way of a picture, for the words do the work that really matters. Nursery rhymes are primarily verbal experiences, and there can surely be no better way of introducing young children to the riches of their mother tongue than through sharing with them the magnificent nursery rhyme tradition.

Nevertheless, from the eighteenth century onward, nursery rhyme books have been taken as a natural province for book illustrators and, as Iona and Peter Opie's recent splendid exhibition at the National Book League showed, the genre has attracted a huge variety of graphic styles. * It is not the purpose of the present display to try to duplicate even the contemporary items from that exhibition, but rather to assert the dangers that arise when an oral art is taken over by graphic artists. As we shall also see in the Section below on Folk Tales and Fairy Tales, pre-eminence here justly belongs to the word rather than the image and (despite the exceptional example of a book like *Ride a Cock-Horse* (77))it behoves the illustrator to act in a supportive rather than a domineering capacity. He must be sensitive both to the demands of his text and the best traditions of its illustration, where (as, supremely, in Caldecott) simplicity, humour and narrative content are paramount.

(66) **Treasury of Nursery Rhymes** compiled by Hilda Boswell *Collins* n.d. [1966] 95p.
One of the most widely sold of contemporary collections, this volume probably does more than most to confirm the popular view of nursery rhymes as something from the land of Bluebell Fairies. Its apparently 'traditional' style is not true to the tradition of the poetry but only to that of the mass-produced children's book ; it has about as much sense of the past as tea-shoppe architecture.

The major objection to the *Treasury*, however (and it is one which applies to the following three examples) is that it may preempt the child's imaginative response to the rhymes, so that for him the romanticism of 'Lavender's Blue' or the rough-and-tumble of 'Goosey Gander' will forever be associated with Hilda Boswell's tepid pictures. Her weak draughtsmanship and complete lack of imaginative sympathy for the rhymes is paralleled by her cavalier treatment of texts. Verses by Edward Lear are nowhere acknowledged and long rhymes like 'Oranges and Lemons' and 'The House that Jack Built' are cut off in their prime once the end of the page-opening is reached.

*Footnote : See their catalogue *Three Centuries of Nursery Rhymes and Poetry For Children* (Bibliography item 48), for details of the huge range of nursery rhyme books (and associated ephemera) that have proved such a permanent boon to publishers and other entrepreneurs.

(67) Dean's New Gift Book of Nursery Rhymes
illustrated by Janet and Anne Grahame Johnstone *Dean*
1971, 60p.
A shorter, more 'modern' equivalent of the foregoing
treasury. The draughtsmanship is tighter, the colouring
sharper but there is no intuitive sympathy for the wit or
poetry of the rhymes. Once again several rhymes are
sharply curtailed for no apparent reason.

(68) A First Ladybird Book of Nursery Rhymes
illustrated by Frank Hampson *Ladybird Books* 1965, 15p.
(69) A Little Poppet Book of Rhymes illustrated by
Norman T. Stephenson *Dean* 1967, o.p.
Two very cheap nursery rhyme books exemplifying the
mass-market style of production. The Ladybird book,
however, has one unusual feature in its wide variations in
the treatment of subjects. Its pictures change
disconcertingly in their detail ('Little Bo Peep' and 'Baa Baa
Black Sheep'), in their approach to perspective ('Little Miss
Muffet' and 'Hickory Dickory Dock') and in their period
setting ('This Little Pig Went to Market', 'Wee Willie
Winkie' and 'I Love Little Pussy').

(70) Best Nursery Rhymes Ever by Richard Scarry
Hamlyn, 1971, 90p. (NY, *Western* 1964).
What distinguishes Richard Scarry's avowedly 'popular'
collection from the foregoing is, first, his far more individual
style and, second, his keen sense of the kind of rhyme to
which it is suited. The huge pictures and their bold
colouring do tend to swamp the small verses, and
unnecessarily so when, as in 'One Misty Moisty Morning'
for instance, not much is going on. But in action-scenes like
'Elsie Marley' or 'There Was an Old Woman who Lived in a
Shoe' Scarry's enjoyment of bustle brings in a
complementary element of fun.

(71) Lavender's Blue a book of nursery rhymes compiled
by Kathleen Lines and pictured by Harold Jones *Oxford
University Press* n.d. [1954] £2·00.
If an interpretation of 'the tradition of the poetry' (66
above) is sought, there can be few happier examples of it
than *Lavender's Blue*. The wide-ranging and carefully
edited selection of rhymes is matched by illustrations that
are constantly sensitive to the spirit of the verse. Very often
much of the page – whether in colour or monochrome – will
be occupied by the picture, but because of intelligent
design, muted shading and a respect for narrative content
they do not obtrude upon the rhymes but chime with them.
Harold Jones's individual style – the rustic scenes and the
simple doll-like figures – help to sustain the sense of the
nursery rhyme in a world of toys.

(72) Ring-a-Ring o' Roses illustrated by Raymond
Briggs *Hamish Hamilton* 1962, £1·40.

(73) The White Land: a picture book of nursery rhymes
illustrated by Raymond Briggs *Hamish Hamilton* 1963,
£1·40.

(74) Fee-fi-fo-fum: a picture book of traditional rhymes
and verses *Hamish Hamilton* 1964, £1·25.

(75) The Mother Goose Treasury illustrated by
Raymond Briggs *Hamish Hamilton* 1966, £3·25.
A sequence of interpretations by one artist, rich in

possibilities for discussion. From the first volume onwards,
Raymond Briggs has shown himself to be resourceful in his
choice of texts (the final two books acknowledge a debt to
Iona and Peter Opie) and this in itself bespeaks a pleasure in
and an affection for his chosen subjects. What is of moment,
however, is the way in which his illustrative style has moved
away from the warmth of *Ring-a-Ring o' Roses* (whose
only fault, surely, is the extended and therefore unrhythmic
treatment accorded to 'Jack and Jill') to the sharpness of
the *Treasury*.

If one accepts a view of the nursery rhyme as a nursery
(rather than a social or historical) phenomenon, then there
is much to be regretted in this shift of style. Raymond
Briggs's three earlier and smaller collections, despite their
evolving manner, all acknowledged the distinctive humour
or feeling of their contributory rhymes and were very much
unified wholes. The *Treasury*, on the other hand, has
sacrificed a single standpoint (such as characterised Harold
Jones's work in *Lavender's Blue*) in favour of a kind of
graphic opportunism. It is at its best in some of the smaller
jokes and riddles, but for much of the book it manifests
itself in crude and often inappropriate draughtsmanship
(compare his 'Oranges and Lemons' with that by Harold
Jones) and harsh, coarsely printed colours.

(76) Mother Goose by Brian Wildsmith *Oxford
University Press* 1964, £1·50.
A curiously static, and finally boring, assemblage by
another widely renowned illustrator. The repetitious page
layouts, with the rhymes so often appearing centred below
the picture, contribute to the book's lack of vitality;
fundamentally, though, the weakness lies in Brian
Wildsmith's failure to catch the dynamic movement of the
rhymes. In very simple pieces like 'Dickery, dickery, dare' or
'A Wise Old Owl' his portrait approach has succeeded in
summarising the content of the stanza, but as soon as the
least narrative enters, or the least 'character development',
his pictures block the imagination rather than assist it.
What a frustrating 'Humpty Dumpty' at the start, for
instance; what a lost opportunity in 'Goosey Gander' – and
even when a 'total action' is portrayed as in 'This Little Pig
Went to Market' what a muddle of events.

(77) Ride a Cock-Horse and other nursery rhymes
illustrated by Mervyn Peake *Chatto & Windus* 1940,
reprinted 1972, £1·25.
Here too a certain formalism in the presentation prevails –
each rhyme faced by its companion illustration. In so small
a collection, however, such a regular pattern gives the book
a necessary unity, and in any case the imagination working
within these illustrations supplies an energy far beyond
anything that Brian Wildsmith could manage in *Mother
Goose* (76) (Compare those fine ladies on their
cock-horses, those Old King Coles, those luckless
Dr Fosters). Mervyn Peake's view of nursery rhymes has
none of the homeliness of *Lavender's Blue* (71) or of the
two volumes that are described below, but it flows from an
intensive reading of and response to the chosen rhymes and
as such (and most unusually) raises the stature of these
little verses to a new imaginative level. Even where, as in
'I Saw a Ship a-sailing', he uses only part of the rhyme, he
contrives to imbue it with a new and inexplicable sense of
mystery (see Mervyn Peake's statements on the art of
drawing. Bibliography items 50 and 51).

(78) **Father Fox's Pennyrhymes** by Clyde Watson, illustrated by Wendy Watson *Macmillan* 1972, £1·50. (NY, *Crowell*, 1971).
Not a nursery rhyme book in the strictest sense, because all the 'pennyrhymes' are original. But the writing catches the lilt and timbre of the tradition to perfection and the illustrations are an inspired demonstration of how the tradition may be captured in pictures. The busy scenes, the rhymes and exchanges that go on in conversation bubbles, the subtle use of strip-cartoon and broken-picture all combine to provide children with one of those rare picture books that 'deserve to be hugged forever'.

(79) **Lullabies and Night Songs** edited by William Engvick, music by Alec Wilder, pictures by Maurice Sendak *Bodley Head* 1969, £2·25. (NY, *Harper & Row*, 1965).
Also not strictly a nursery rhyme book, but an unusual attempt to combine words and music within what is essentially a picture book (contrast Walter Crane's method in the item 85 below). As it happens, the music is not entirely satisfactory, but the choice and sequence of lullabies is original and the illustrations form a courteous and beautifully conceived acknowledgement by Maurice Sendak to the illustrators of the past who have influenced him: William Blake and Samuel Palmer, Ludwig Richter and Randolph Caldecott. These masters are prefigured in headpieces, tailpieces and full-scale pictures which are nonetheless inimitable Sendak.

Comparisons from the Past

Beside the wealth displayed in *Three Centuries of Nursery Rhymes and Poetry for Children* (Bibliography item 48) these few collections are ludicrously unrepresentative. They merely indicate one or two varied ways of displaying the rhymes in pictures.

(80) **Nursery Songs** *Frederick Warne* n.d. [?1865] (Aunt Louisa's London Toy Books).
A popular mid-nineteenth century presentation, printed by Kronheim. About this time there was a fashion for black backgrounds, giving a feeling that all events took place in everlasting night.

(81) **Child's Play** by E. V. B(oyle). *Sampson Low*, 1866.
An edition of a collection first published in 1852, here illustrated with an almost Pre-Raphaelite splendour.

(82) **Mother Goose,** or the Old Nursery Rhymes. Illustrated by Kate Greenaway. *George Routledge & Sons.* n.d. [1881].
Perhaps the best example of Kate Greenaway's art and a triumph of colour printing by Edmund Evans (see his *Reminiscences*, Bibliograpy item 57, page 65). The book is still in print (and has even been recently issued in a German edition, *Mutter Gans* Insel 1973) but it is a mere ghost of its former self. In his *Mother Goose's Garnishings* (Bibliography item 47) Maurice Sendak refers to the book as 'this lovely but antiseptic affair' — 'the great ancestor of the sentimental Mother Goose books'.

(83) **Familiar Rhymes from Mother Goose,** with new pictures by Chester Loomis. *Ernest Nister*, 1888.
An extraordinarily forward-looking graphic style, the more

surprising as coming from a publisher noted for his wholly undistinguished (but often impressively lithographed) gift-books.

(84) **Nursery Rhymes,** with pictures by C. Lovat Fraser. *T. C. and E. C. Jack.* n.d. [?1921].
A bold twentieth century treatment, not too distant in style from the work of Mervyn Peake.

(85) **The Baby's Opera**: a book of old rhymes with new dresses, by Walter Crane. *George Routledge & Sons.* n.d. [1877].
A decorative treatment of words and music that contrasts with the later:

(86) **Little Songs of Long Ago** . . . Illustrated by Willebeek Le Mair. *Augener Ltd.* etc. n.d. [1912].

6a. INDIVIDUAL NURSERY RHYMES

Alongside the large illustrated compendia there are many picture books which have been created from one or two nursery rhymes only (a practice which dates back at least to John Harris's famous edition of *Old Mother Hubbard* in 1805). Without doubt the most famous exponent of this style of presentation was Randolph Caldecott, whose individual 'toy books' were published at a rate of some two a year from 1878 until his death in 1886. These are still available (albeit in much inferior printings) either as single volumes or in bound collections, two of which are included here in order to show first Caldecott's unerring ability to 'pace' the rhymes from page to page and second his still unsurpassed command of line and composition in the service of his narrative.

(87) **The Three Jovial Huntsmen** by Randolph Caldecott, *Warne* 50p.

(88) Randolph Caldecott's **Second Collection of Pictures & Songs** *Warne* n.d. [1935] £1·85.
Beside Caldecott's fluid and richly humorous toy books many of our present day nursery rhyme picture books seem stiff and unresponsive ; note, for instance, the heavy animal portraiture in :

(89) **Who Killed Cock-Robin ?** a picture book by Maureen Roffey, *Bodley Head* 1971, £1·05.

or the fussy and pallid drawing in :

(90) **I Saw A Ship A-Sailing** pictures by Janina Domanska, *Hamish Hamilton* 1973, £1·40. (NY, *Macmillan*, 1972).
a book outshone by a single page opening in Mervyn Peake's *Ride a Cock-Horse* (77).

Something of Caldecott's abundant wit does however appear in :

(91) **The House that Jack Built** pictures by Paul Galdone *Bodley Head* 1962, 80p. (NY, *McGraw-Hill* 1961).
a comedy which, like Caldecott's, needs no highly coloured emphasis to make the most of the jokes in the story.
Compare it with Rodney Peppé's version :

(92) **The House that Jack Built** illustrated by Rodney Peppé *Longman Young Books* 1970, £1·20.
which is flat and stolid for all its brightness.

A similar light-heartedness pervades :

(93) **Old Mother Hubbard and her Dog** pictures by Paul Galdone *Bodley Head* 1961, 58p. (NY, *McGraw-Hill* 1960).
the artist and his dog George co-operating with a vivacity that overcomes the inherent repetitiousness of the verses — so much more obvious in the too contrived pages of :

(94) **Old Mother Hubbard and her Dog** illustrated by Evaline Ness *Longman Young Books* 1973, £1·10.

or the original but over-cumbersome designs of :

(95) **The Comic Adventures of Old Mother Hubbard and her Dog** illustrations by Arnold Lobel *Collins* 1970, 60p. (NY, *Bradbury* 1968).

The most imaginative and the most determinedly original treatments accorded to short traditional rhymes are perhaps those in :

(96) **Hector Protector and As I Went Over the Water** two nursery rhymes with pictures by Maurice Sendak *Bodley Head* 1967, £1·05. (NY, *Harper* 1965).

and in :

(97) **Willy O'Dwyer Jumped in the Fire** variations on a folk rhyme by Beatrice Schenk De Regniers, illustrated by Beni Montresor. *Collins* 1970, o.p. (NY, *Atheneum* 1968).
Sendak, with his deep appreciation of Caldecott, catches most completely the spirit of the two brief rhymes — which are amazingly sustained through pages of pictures unaccompanied by text ; Montresor, despite his modishness, the obscurity of his red panels and his debt to Sendak in the matter of conversation bubbles ('Help !'), is nonetheless highly stimulating in his theatrical interpretation of the text.

Comparisons from the Past

(98) **The Adventures of Old Mother Hubbard and her Comical Dog** part II *John Bysh* n.d.
A 'Harris' style publication using hand-coloured woodcut illustrations.

(99) **An Elegy on the Death and Burial of Cock Robin.** Ornamented with cuts. York, *J. Kendrew*. n.d. [c1820].
A famous chapbook edition.

(100) **The Complete and Wonderful History of Cock Robin and Jenny Wren** *Dean & Son*. n.d. [c.1855].
A cheaply produced, hand-coloured edition whose 'realistic' portrayals contrast sharply with the modern paintings by Maureen Roffey (item 89).

(101) **The Fairy Ship** *George Routledge & Sons* n.d. [1869].
Walter Crane's version of 'I saw a ship a-sailing' (90).

(102) **Sing a Song for Sixpence.** Illustrated by Randolph Caldecott. *George Routledge & Sons.* n.d. [1880].

One page opening from one of 'Caldecott's Picture Books' in an early edition, which will help to show the delicacy of the original printing as against editions currently available. Note too the pictorial references on the Queen's parlour walls, matched on an earlier page by Robinson Crusoe and Jack-the-Giant-Killer in the King's counting house.

7. SIMPLE STORIES

Alongside nursery-rhyme picture books there is also a place for those simple picture story-books which may give young children their first experience of the told story. Unlike most of the domestic tales discussed above in Section 4, the impulse behind the best of these story-books is literary and artistic rather than descriptive. The author and his illustrator (very often combined in one and the same person) are free to establish any relationship they choose between word and picture, and where they have found the right balance they may produce books of great aesthetic satisfaction (to adults and children alike).

There should be no hard and fast distinction drawn here between 'original' storybooks and the picture versions of simple traditional tales which are discussed in Section 11 below, but because of some special factors which arise in the criticism of the latter an artificial division has been made for the purposes of this exhibition.

Similarly it is not altogether proper that these books should be divorced from those in Section 8 — especially since the thesis there set out depends upon the recognition of qualities of liveliness, humour and artistry which are common to the best in both sections. However, because of the essentially purposive nature of books designed for children learning to read, there is a tendency for illustration to be seen as something explanatory of or supplementary to the text in a way which is less demanding imaginatively than in many of the following examples. Indeed, in the best of these simple story-books, the integration of text and picture is managed with such natural ease that, critically speaking, it is impossible to assess the one without taking account of the other. Here, more than anywhere else in the exhibition, the art of the picture book is to be seen at its purest.

(103) **Bedtime for Frances** by Russell Hoban, pictures by Garth Williams *Faber* 1963, £1·00. (NY, *Harper* 1960).
Russell Hoban's stories about Frances the badger link across to those books like *Lucy and Tom's Day* (51) which take their character from their treatment of family life. Nearly all the 'Frances books' have for their theme some small domestic crisis (here it is fear of the dark) which is resolved through a good-humoured tolerance which allows the child himself to understand the situation. Russell Hoban's pert text and Garth Williams's comfortable pictures sustain the book on a knife edge between sentimentality and moralising. Furthermore, by humanising a family of badgers, Russell Hoban is able to write of generalised domestic situations with which the child reader may have a fuller sympathy than he does with such essays on everyday family life as the similarly skilful :

(104) **Herman the Loser** by Russell Hoban, pictures by Lillian Hoban *World's Work* 1972, £1·00. (NY, *Harper* 1961).

Just how successful the unemphatic Hobans are can be shown by comparing their family stories with such overtly moralistic domestic tales as these :

(105) **The Hating Book** by Charlotte Zolotow, pictures by Ben Shecter *World's Work* 1971, o.p. (NY, *Harper* 1969) ; and :
(106) **The Shy Little Girl** by Phyllis Krasilovsky, illustrated by Trina Schart Hyman *World's Work* 1971, £1·05. (Boston, *Houghton* 1970).
The highly skilled execution of the illustrations cannot do more than moderate the authors' didactic intentions.

(107) **Whistle for Willie** by Ezra Jack Keats *Bodley Head* 1966, 95p. (NY, *Viking Press*, 1964).
The first, and perhaps the most successful, of a series of books which take the boy Peter through small childhood crises similar to those which beset Frances the badger. Ezra Jack Keats's bright collages though are radically different in style from Lillian Hoban's pen and brush work for the later 'Frances' books, replacing her homeliness with a more formal manner, which distances the book a little from the reader.

(108) **Harry the Dirty Dog** by Gene Zion, illustrated by Margaret Bloy Graham *Bodley Head* 1960, 75p. (NY, *Harper* 1956).
A justly famous dog story, whose self-effacing illustrations achieve their effect by their commitment simply to portraying the story and to sustaining through it the character of the unforgettable Harry.

(109) **Angus and the Ducks** told and pictured by Marjorie Flack *Bodley Head* 1933, 70p. (NY, *Doubleday* n.d.).
Yet another dog story, and one which, like *Harry* (108), subordinates graphic elaboration to the demands of the story. There is, however, much skill in the way text and picture are balanced on each page, and in the handling of the pages that lead up to the climax and, afterwards, settle back to echo the 'sofa' motif of the opening. The five 'Angus' books of which this is the first appeared originally in the United States from 1930 onwards.

(110) **Rosie's Walk** by Pat Hutchins *Bodley Head* 1968, £1·00. (NY, *Macmillan* 1968).
A fine example of the illustrator putting all the drama of her story into the pictures, while the simple text proceeds on a course as innocent of guile as that of Rosie herself. The flat, stylised manner gives scope for more comic effect than at first seems possible, demanding that the 'reader' look carefully as each scene is set up and demolished.

(111) **The Rain Puddle** by Adelaide Holl, pictures by Roger Duvoisin *Bodley Head* 1966, 90p. (NY, *Lothrop, Lee & Shepard*, 1965).
Another farm-yard joke, which leaves the reader to enjoy the point without too much fuss. The flat patterns of the pictures allow for some attractive colour composition and simplify the job of portraying reflections in water.

(112) **The Sly Old Cat** by Beatrix Potter *Warne* 1971, 60p.
(113) **The Story of Miss Moppet** by Beatrix Potter *Warne* 1906, 40p.
(114) **The Story of a Fierce Bad Rabbit** by Beatrix Potter *Warne* 1906, 40p.
The fame of *Peter Rabbit* (297) has sometimes prevented an

appreciation of Beatrix Potter's neat handling of even smaller tales. Each of these three texts was planned as a 'panorama' rather than a hinged book, and a restoration of them to that form (see items 136 and 137) exemplifies even better the strength and sharp humour running through both text and pictures. See L. Linder *A History of the Writings of Beatrix Potter* (Bibliography item 57). pp 182–4 and accompanying plates which show a facsimile of the manuscript of *The Sly Old Cat*.

(115) **Clever Bill** by William Nicholson, new edition *Faber* 1958, o.p.
(116) **The Pirate Twins** by William Nicholson *Faber* 1929, o.p.
Sir William Nicholson's only two picture stories for children, but each is exemplary in its artistic control. The integration of text and picture is determined absolutely by the use of hand-written and not printed script, so that Nicholson is able to plan each story as a rhythmic unit. Despite their brevity, these stories have a concreteness about them which sorts well with the imaginative and highly personal illustrations. * First published in 1926 and 1929, these books are some of the earliest examples in England of the use of colour offset lithography for 'trade' picture books.

(117) **In the Forest** by Marie Hall Ets *Faber* 1967, 80p. (NY, *Viking*, 1944).
Reverses the Nicholson coin. Instead of the spare text and expansive illustrations, here is a 'story' whose carefully wrought phrases develop an elaborate series of verbal rhythms. Even so, the words have been carefully wedded to the picture sequence, whose monochrome tones interfere less than colour would have done with the pre-eminent text.

The text of *In the Forest* also introduces the device of cumulation, which is found so often in traditional nursery tales (eg : items 225 and 227) and whose build-ups and repetitions exert such an appeal on the young child. It is the cumulative stripping of Sambo by the tigers that gives the impetus to :

(118) **The Story of Little Black Sambo** by Helen Bannerman *Chatto & Windus* 1899, 40p.
and that makes the tigers' dissolution and the final distribution of pancakes so eminently satisfying. The artlessness of the tale and of its accompanying home-made illustrations has been much criticised of late as enshrining a crude and paternalistic attitude towards coloured families. For all that, there is no escaping that Mrs. Bannerman's little story has an immediacy of appeal which has nothing to do with the names or life-style of its protagonist and everything to do with dramatic shape and unpretentious language. Despite great charm, such immediacy is less evident in another 'tiger' book :

*Footnote : It is noteworthy that Maurice Sendak acknowledges in his introduction to item 124, the influence of *The Pirate Twins* on *Where the Wild Things Are* (123) while Wanda Gág 'wanted the shape of *Millions of Cats* to be the same as Nicolson's (sic) *Clever Bill*, which was both small book and large one'. (See Bibliography item 39, p. 36).

(119) **Tot Botot and his Little Flute** by Laura Cathon, pictures by Arnold Lobel *Longman Young Books* 1972, 70p. (NY, *Macmillan* 1970).
Here professionalism is evident in every line, both of text and drawing. The rhythms of the composition are faultless and the book is as captivating as Tot Botot's flute itself – but there is no 'ghee', and no pancakes.

Provocative of no-one (unless perhaps grocers or barrow boys) is :

(120) **The Elephant and the Bad Baby** by Elfrida Vipont, illustrated by Raymond Briggs *Hamish Hamilton* 1969, £1·25.
where flutes are replaced by trumpetings and where the cumulative principle works to perfection, both in the quasi 'Gingerbread Man' chase and in Raymond Briggs's portrayal of it and of its sudden, cataclysmic end.

The supplementing, during the chase, of colour work with line drawing represents the continuance of a method of narrative illustration that Randolph Caldecott made very much his own and that has been used in another cumulative picture book worthy of that master himself :

(121) **Mr Gumpy's Outing** by John Burningham *Cape* 1970, £1·05.
The gradual pile-up of creatures in Mr Gumpy's boat, the inevitable disaster and the concluding tea-party have a naturalness in both the telling and the illustration which goes a long way to support the claim that perfection in picture books is not to be sought in the predominance of one element over another but in the easy interlocking of all the parts.

Few illustrators have a better appreciation of this than Maurice Sendak, whose every book offers some especial felicity in the marrying of text and picture. Two of his finest achievements are :

(122) **Mr Rabbit and the Lovely Present** by Charlotte Zolotow, illustrated by Maurice Sendak *Bodley Head* 1968, 90p. (NY, *Harper & Row*, 1962).
not quite a cumulative tale, but one whose repetition of conversational exchanges requires sensitive illustration if it is not to appear absurd. As it is, Maurice Sendak gives the words a setting and the characters a personality which is completely winning and which produces, as the 'story' proceeds, a marvellous sense of warmth and friendliness. (As one reviewer said when the book first appeared in England 'A lovely present indeed'.)

The second book is Maurice Sendak's celebrated :

(123) **Where the Wild Things Are** *Bodley Head* 1967, £1·25. (NY, *Harper* 1963).
arguments about the contents of which have tended to cloud appreciation of its graphic versatility. The enthusiastic faction have perhaps overstated some of their claims for the book (Max, for instance, is hardly a very sympathetic hero figure) but it should be hard for their opponents to deny the skill with which the progress of the story is reflected in its illustration (the progression in size of the pictures, the 'wild rumpus' sequence) and – in its quieter printings – the delicacy of the draughtsmanship and colour work.

Because of the variety of editions which it has been possible to obtain, and because of the illustrator's known concern for the quality with which his work is reproduced, this book is a good example of the variations which willy-nilly creep into colour printing. In addition to the book on the open stands, there are also displayed the first American, first British, first Japanese and first Puffin paperback editions, all open at the same page in order to show the colour variations. As a 'control', there is also shown a printing of the same picture prepared under Maurice Sendak's own supervision and incorporated as an item in :

(124) **Pictures by Maurice Sendak** *Bodley Head* 1972, £13·00. + VAT (NY, *Harper* 1971).
A portfolio of some of the pictures which the artist 'likes the best', and which have been individually printed. Other illustrations are shown in proximity to items 79, 96, 122, and 345.

One result of the publication of *Where the Wild Things Are* was its imitation. It unleashed a profusion of monsters upon the reading population and such books as :

(125) **The Monster's Visit** by Beman Lord, illustrated by Don Bolognese *Hamish Hamilton* 1968, o.p. (NY, *Walck* 1967) ;
(126) **The Fourteenth Dragon** by James E. Seidelman *Harlin Quist*, distributed in the UK by *W. H. Allen* n.d. £1·05.
(127) **Henry and the Monstrous Din** by Russell Hoban, pictures by Lillian Hoban, *World's Work*, 1967, o.p. latched on to the automatic attraction that strange beasts have for the child's imagination, but without the spontaneity of Mr Sendak's book.

Much the most satisfying of the 'Wild Things' imitations (if indeed it is one since its naturalness bespeaks independent creation) is :
(128) **The Judge** by Harve and Margot Zemach *Bodley Head* 1970, £1·05. (NY, *Farrar, Straus & Giroux*, 1969).
a book with a graphic style and a sense of caricature very similar to Sendak's own, and one where – as the final rumpus begins – words once more give way to a completely visual interpretation.

Comparisons from the Past

(129) **The Butterfly's Ball and the Grasshopper's Feast** by Mr. Roscoe printed for J. Harris 1808.
A 'story' in verse, illustrated after drawings by William Mulready. Text and illustration are engraved together on a single printing plate and the picture hand-coloured after printing – a style commonly used by John Harris and other publishers at this period.

(130) **The Peacock 'At Home'** by a Lady [ie : Catherine Ann Dorset] Twenty-second edition, *Grant & Griffith* 1844.
The first of many imitations of William Roscoe's highly successful poem appearing here thirty-seven years after the first edition, with hand-coloured engravings and nature notes.

(131) W. Belch's **Butterfly's Ball** printed and sold by W. Belch n.d. [c1820].
A more heavily coloured competitor to the 'standard' Harris edition. Recent adaptations of the poem for adults have been excluded from the exhibition.

(132) **The Robins**: a family history. *Frederick Warne & Co.* n.d. [c.1870].

(133) **Goody Two Shoes** *George Routledge & Sons* n.d. [1874] (Walter Crane's Toy Books, shilling series).
Heavily abridged Victorian editions of two eighteenth century 'classics', where it would seem that the well-known titles have been used as a commercial draw, giving an air of respectability to the dominating pictures.

(134) **The Three Little Kittens.** *Nelson.* n.d. [c.1870].
What little story there is here is simply an excuse for showing off the almost *coup l'oeil* detail of the lithographed illustrations.

(135) **How Jessie Was Lost.** *George Routledge & Sons.* n.d. [1868]. (Routledge's New Sixpenny Toy Books, No. 69).
A little adventure in verse (hardly comparable, however, with the child adventures of Mr Ardizzone's Tim, 288-9) illustrated by Walter Crane in a more 'realistic' vein than usual.

(136) **The Story of Miss Moppet** by Beatrix Potter. *Frederick Warne & Co.* n.d. [1906].

(137) **The Story of a Fierce Bad Rabbit** by Beatrix Potter. *Frederick Warne & Co.* n.d. [1906].
Panoramic versions, exhibited for contrast with items 113 and 114.

8. AT THE POINT OF READING

Some might feel that books devised to instruct children in the art of reading should have no place in this exhibition. Their manufacturers do not submit them to the world as picture books and the educationists who promote or discuss them always see them in total isolation from all the other books that surround young children. It is almost as though 'learning to read' has nothing to do with enjoying books at all.

To anyone less preoccupied with education than educationists or the concocters of reading-schemes, it should however be clear that the planned series is only part of a much wider context. A child lucky enough to live with books like *Father Fox's Pennyrhymes* (78) or *Mr Gumpy's Outing* (121) will (rightly) be bringing certain expectations to bear on the books he meets when learning to read ; and the child unlucky enough to have met with no books at all before this stage will need some persuasion as to the rewards of the task he is about. If a single quality can be adduced which may meet the expectations of the one, or the need for conviction of the other, then that quality is vigour. The way words are used, the rhythm with which a text develops, the opportunities taken for jokes and conversational inflections must be related to the child's natural pleasure in the direct, the forceful and the comic. Similarly a pleasure in the play of words, a desire to read on, may be stimulated or enhanced by illustrations which reflect the vigour of the text.

Only on rare occasions – *Little Bear* (144) ; *Inside Outside Upside Down* (148) – is it likely that word and picture will chime with the easy naturalness that characterizes the 'pure' picture book. The inhibitions of producing a book, or set of books, to a purpose are too great. Nevertheless, the following examples give evidence of the variety of methods that have been devised to try to lighten the learner's task.

(138) **Play With Us** by W. Murray, illustrated by J. H. Wingfield *Ladybird Books* 1964, 15p.
The first book in a reading-scheme which has not only met with the approval of many educationists, but which (unlike many of its competitors) is widely on sale to the general public. The lack of any direction in the text and its unnatural phrasing is matched by the posed, 'family snapshot' style of the pictures.

(139) **Doing the Pools** by Leila Berg, illustrated by Richard Rose *Macmillan* 1972, 9p.
In an endeavour to escape from the constricting formulae of the reading-scheme, Leila Berg is editing the two series of 'Little Nippers' and 'Nippers' in which an element of control over vocabulary and sentence difficulty is exercised, but without (in the most successful examples) abandoning a strong feeling for speech rhythms and slapstick humour. *Doing the Pools* shows how a neatly turned text can gain in impact and enjoyment through illustrations whose rough and ready style matches the air of colloquialism, and whose colour and use of the small square page admirably complements the story's narrative momentum.

A similarly successful joint volume is :

(140) **Fish and Chips for Supper** by Leila Berg, pictures by Richard Rose. *Macmillan* 1968, 15p.
in the Red (easiest) Group of 'big' 'Nippers'.

(141) **My Mum** by David Mackay, Brian Thompson and Pamela Schaub, illustrated by John Dyke *Penguin:* A Breakthrough Reading Book 1973, 12p. (*Longman* 1970). A comparison of the text of this school reader (which has been converted into a 'trade' book) with that of *Doing the Pools* (139) provides support for the argument that a committee cannot write books so well as an individual author. The dull, static sentences are also matched by dull, static illustrations, whose modish use of colour and perspective have none of the easy-natured freedom of those by Richard Rose. Bigness (page 2) is certainly in evidence, but hardly prettiness (page 3). (See also item 54 above).

(142) **Rug is a Bear** by Helen Cresswell, illustrated by Susanna Gretz *Benn:* First Steps in Reading Series 1968, 40p.
One of the bears from item 39 has escaped into this series, giving it an imaginative and humorous appeal denied to the more solemn 'boy-house-tree' readers. The idea of asking a 'creative' rather than an 'educational' writer to work within the limitations of a controlled vocabulary has certainly produced a text of greater flexibility than often occurs (but not so great as that by Leila Berg in 'Little Nippers' (139) or the Berenstains in 'Beginning Beginners' (148ff)) ; without Susanna Gretz's Rug, however, the series would be much the poorer.

(143) **A House for Jones** by Helen Cresswell, illustrated by Margaret Gordon *Benn:* Beginning to Read Series 1969, 45p.
An example from a long series which leads on from more formal reading schemes or from such preliminary series as 'First Steps in Reading' (142 above). 'Beginning to Read' books are notable for the extent to which they have, from the start, commissioned illustrations from such widely respected artists as Val Biro, Margery Gill and Shirley Hughes. Understandably, therefore, the result has been itself respectable – but has demonstrated to perfection how,

with the best will in the world, an element of the mechanical creeps into writing and illustration done to order. In *A House for Jones*, for instance, Helen Cresswell offers a text which tries hard to catch, but falls short of, the easygoing rhythm of a folk-tale (so well caught in a book like *Mr Rabbit and the Lovely Present* (122)), and Margaret Gordon responds with illustrations that, for all their brightness and flexible use of pages, lack character and narrative pace.

(144) Little Bear by Else Holmelund Minarik, pictures by Maurice Sendak *World's Work:* I-can-read Series 1958, 85p. (NY, *Harper* 1957).
The first of an American series planned with similar intentions to those of 'Beginning to Read' books. While many stories in this much more extensive series suffer from a slightly self-conscious working to normative rules, *Little Bear* shows how it is possible for an author and illustrator, working in harmony, to produce a book which transcends the limited intention of the series. Mrs Minarik's text hangs uneasily between the colloquial and the sentimental throughout, but is saved from excess by the carefully integrated illustrations, which match the cosiness of the mother-child relationship but bring a necessary touch of movement and humour. An equally attractive 'I-can-read' book is :

(145) Frog and Toad are Friends by Arnold Lobel *World's Work:* I-can-read Series 1971, 95p. (NY, *Harper* 1970).
where an author/illustrator contributes a little group of gently humorous stories, the warmth of whose text is inseparable from that of the accompanying pictures.

(146) Ant and Bee: an alphabetical story for tiny tots by Angela Banner, illustrations by Bryan Ward *Kaye & Ward* 1950, 40p.
First and most popular of a popular series, which seeks to bring play methods into a story designed to teach. Such are the contrivances in *Ant and Bee* to construct a story on stepping-stones (each stone being a three-letter word beginning with a new letter of the alphabet) that, without its visual attractiveness, the book would be sheer inconsequence. As it is however, the small format, the clear, simple pictures on every page opening, and the device of printing all the stepping-stone words in red, so that the child can call them out as they arrive, serve to involve him with the book as with a toy.

(147) My Aunt's Alphabet with Billy and Me by Charlotte Hough *Penguin: Puffin* 1969, 22½p.
Employing a method of isolating words through the alphabet rather as Angela Banner does, Charlotte Hough produces here a series of incidents with a similar rather absurd inconsequence. There is a striking contrast between the Note and the Index, which deal with the author's policy over vocabulary, and the colourful informality of her illustrations.

Beginning Beginner and **Beginner Books** by Dr Seuss *Collins*
For all the earnestness and good-will that have gone into many of the foregoing examples in this section, none of them has quite managed to combine simplicity with panache in the way that the 'Dr Seuss' books do. There are at present over sixty books in the two 'Beginner' series and it is only natural that there should be much variation in their quality ; at their best, however, they exhibit an ebullience

and a verbal dexterity which not only seems more natural than many contrived, vocabulary-controlled books but which also accords with the child's love of the rumbustious and the funny.

It is these qualities that predominate in the illustrations. The graphic work of such regular contributors to the series as the Berenstains, Roy McKie and Dr Seuss (or, sometimes, Theo Le Sieg) himself may differ in points of detail — firmness of outline, for instance, or opacity and disposition of colour — but it shares the common characteristics of being frankly populist. It owes its debts of influence to the traditions of the child's comic and the cartoon film rather than to those of the illustrated book (even though like crudities and exaggerations have been present in children's picture books at least from the time of *Struwwelpeter* (335) or *The Complete Nonsense* (21)).

From the huge roster of 'Beginner Books' examples have been chosen here which exhibit the linking of word and picture at its best in the various stages of the series :

(148) Inside Outside Upside Down by Stan and Jan Berenstain *Collins* : Bright and Early 'Beginning Beginners' 1969, 60p. (NY, *Random House*, 1968).
A *tour de force:* a nursery comedy using only twenty-three different words, but getting a pace and rhythm out of them that puts all the manufactured readers to shame. The fun of the text, though, is immensely enhanced by that of the illustration — not only in such obvious extras as the tree house, but also in details like the comic expressiveness of the eyes peering from the box.

Other notable successes of this author/artist team are :

(149) Old Hat New Hat by Stan and Jan Berenstain *Collins* 1971, 60p. (NY, *Random House*, 1970).

(150) The Berenstains' B Book by Stan and Jan Berenstain *Collins* 1972, 60p. NY, (*Random House*, 1971).
both in the 'Beginning Beginner Books' section of the series.

(151) The Eye Book by Theo Le Sieg, illustrated by Roy McKie *Collins* Bright and Early 'Beginning Beginners' 1969, 60p. NY, (*Random House*, 1968).
McKie's looser, washier style tends more than his colleagues' to an unredeemable vulgarity, saved in this instance by the book's implicit satire on reading-scheme methods ; far more exposed in the less spontaneous and longer text of :

(152) The Nose Book by Al Perkins *Collins* Beginning Beginner Series 1971, 60p. (NY, *Random House* 1970).

(153) Marvin K. Mooney will you please go now ! by Dr Seuss *Collins:* Beginning Beginner Series 1973, 60p. (NY, *Random House*, 1972).
A recent and typical example of the native Seuss style, with its quizzical, indeterminate hero, its gallery of self-satisfied creatures and its impossible machines and vehicles. The colours have diversified since the classic experiment that began the series :

(154) The Cat in the Hat by Dr Seuss *Collins:* Beginner Books 1958, 60p. (NY, *Random House*, 1957).
but the vigorous use of the pages is the same, belying the

author/artist's claim to mere amateur status. Note too the resolute refusal to explain too much or to conform to any pre-determined idea of 'reality'. There is a much greater stimulus to the child's imagination in the texts of Dr Seuss than he is often given credit for. See also :

(155) **Mr Brown Can Moo, Can You ?** by Dr Seuss *Collins:* Beginning Beginners 1971, 60p. (NY, *Random House*, 1970).

(156) **Hop on Pop** by Dr Seuss *Collins:* Beginner Books 1964, 60p. (NY, *Random House*, 1963).

(157) **Green Eggs and Ham** by Dr Seuss *Collins:* Beginner Books 1962, 60p. (NY, *Random House*, 1960). and the notes to items 276 and 328.

Comparisons from the Past

(158) **Peter Piper's Practical Principles of Plain and Perfect Pronunciation** to which is added a collection of entertaining conundrums *Grant & Griffith* n.d., [c1857]. Late edition of a popular 'play-way' approach to learning first published by John Harris perhaps as early as 1810.

(159) **The Infant's Toy Book** or pretty tales. Embellished with sixteen neatly coloured engravings. Printed for *A. K. Newman & Co.* n.d. [c1820].
A page showing the rewards of learning to read—the prized prizes of a kite, a ship and a rocking horse. Note the game of cricket in the background.

(160) **Grammar in Rhyme** *George Routledge & Sons* n.d. 1868 (Routledge's New Sixpenny Toybooks, No. 70).
A pictorial approach to grammar illustrated from designs by Walter Crane. Printed on cloth.

(161) **The Mother's Primer** : a little child's first steps in many ways, by Mrs Felix Summerly. With a frontispiece by W(illiam) M(ulready). *Longman, Brown, Green, and Longmans*, 1884.
Not a picture book at all, but a 'home learning' book which attempts by its elegant design, its use of different coloured printing (cf. *Ant and Bee*, item 146) and its activity instructions to make learning to read a pleasurable task. Unlike :

(162) **The English Spelling Book** . . . by William Mavor LLD . . . *George Routledge & Sons*. n.d. [an edition c1900]. Umpteenth edition of one of the most famous primers, here 'revised and brought up to date' by E. H. Montauban MA and incorporating here and there some stock line illustrations. The picture of 'the kid and the wolf' shown here is interesting as having been engraved by John Greenaway, whose daughter was also involved in an edition of the same book :

(163) **The English Spelling Book** . . . by William Mavor LLD. Illustrated by Kate Greenaway. *George Routledge & Sons*, 1885.
Among Kate Greenaway's many line illustrations for the book, all printed in sepia, is this alphabet which was the original of that used in item 32 above.

(164) **The Walter Crane Readers First Primer** by Nellie Dale with pictures by Walter Crane. *J. M. Dent*. n.d. [1899].

A leading craftsman of the day lends his talents to cheering up a 'reader' by one of the period's leading theorists on teaching reading.

9. PICTURES AND PLAY: THE 'ALTERNATIVE BOOK'

It has been argued that one of the reasons why children experience difficulty in learning to read is because books are themselves of no great appeal to young and usually energetic human beings. Faced with the general lack of dynamism in most reading-schemes, such an argument is understandable, and only recently have some teachers come to recognise that the book as a plaything may prove a fillip to rather than a diversion from the child's growth as a reader.

From Victorian times onward, the 'alternative book' has proved a gimmick which has stimulated the ingenuity of publishers and been a cause of subdued amazement or amusement to the public. Progress in the mechanisation of printing methods and book production led to a great variety of cut-out, stand-up, movable and puzzle books upon which the Victorians lavished great technical expertise. Examples from our own day are of rather more humdrum quality, mass production and mass marketing techniques requiring in the main nothing too ornate or too expensive. Our books however do share with most of those of the past a general tendency to subordinate textual and pictorial considerations to the needs of the gimmick which, in view of the natural attractiveness which gimmicks have for children, represents loss of opportunity to develop the child's appreciation of words and pictures.

Pop-Ups

Even in the days of the earliest and most complex pop-up books, text and illustrative style tended to be sacrificed to the ingenuities of the paper constructions. This weakness is even more apparent in our own day where such over-simplified examples as :
(165) **Lucie Attwell's Pop-up Book of Rhymes** *Dean* 1969, o.p.
combines all the weaknesses noted under item 66 with only the crudest of pop-up pictures.

Similarly the many examples of pop-up fairy tales care little for the nature of the material that they are adapting. In :

(166) **Cinderella** *Schlesinger:* Pop-Up Classics 1968, o.p. retold by Albert G. Miller, designed by Paul Taylor, illustrated by Jon Dahlstrom. (NY, *Random House* 1968).
for instance, the writing of the story has been of far less concern than the making of the pop-ups, while :
(167) **Little Red Riding Hood** retold by Christian Willcox, illustrated by Virginia Smith, models designed by Brian Edwards *Blackie* : 'Make Your Own Pop-Up' series 1973, 70p.
lapses into banality in all respects, perhaps from a too-great determination to give the market what it thinks the market expects to receive.

As is noted later under 'Transparent Filters', the most adaptable material for treatment in pop-up form is jokes and riddles. Books like the :

(168) **Pop-Up What Do You Get ?** created by Jack Hanrahan and Phil Hahn. Designed by Paul Taylor. Paper engineering by Tor Lokvig. *Schlesinger* 1969, o.p. succeed admirably. Many of the devices are properly surprising, the jokes have the right air of child-humour about them and the highly coloured graphics, though in the anonymous style of the comic book tradition, have a sufficient character.

(169) **But Where is the Green Parrot ?** by Thomas and Wanda Zacharias *Chatto & Windus* 1968. o.p. (Gütersloh, *Sigbert Mohn* 1965).
A more conventional 'find-it' book, but one whose pictures offer great scope for enjoyment even after the green parrot has been discovered.

Flap Books

(170) **Anybody at Home ?** by H. A. Rey *Chatto & Windus* 1956, 40p. (Boston, *Houghton*, n.d.)
(171) **Feed the Animals** by H. A. Rey *Chatto & Windus* 1956, 40p. (Boston, *Houghton*, n.d.)
(172) **See the Circus** by H. A. Rey *Chatto & Windus* 1956, 40p. (Boston, *Houghton* 1956).
Each flap conceals a guessable surprise, the answer to the rhyme on the facing page. The drawings are simple both in colour and design, often with a humorous and unexpected twist.

(173) **Animal Lore and Disorder** by James Riddell *Atrium* new edition 1973, 65p.
A rather more complex use of the gimmick, enabling the reader not only to create absurd creatures, but also to obtain biological details of uncertain accuracy. With so many combinations possible, there are bound to be a lot of weaknesses, but the 'powerful tail' of the Rhinogaroo and the ferocity of the innocent Torg are nice.

(174) **Ask a Silly Question** by Kent Salisbury, illustrated by Joan Allen *Hamlyn* 1973, 95p. (NY, *Western* 1969).
Carried to extremes, as here, the flap game gets out of hand and becomes merely boring.

Transparent Filters

(175) **Animal Hide-and-Seek** by Annette Tison and Talus Taylor *Warne:* Take Another Look Books 1972, £1·25.

(176) **The Adventures of the Three Colours** by Annette Tison and Talus Taylor *Warne* : Take Another Look Books 1971, £1·25.
The use of transparencies in these stories deprives both the narrative line and the illustration of any real strength, and even the picture-changes rapidly lose their surprise value.

Rather more justification for the gimmick can be found in :
(177) **The Double Colour ABC Book,** illustrated by Richard Fowler *Perpetua Press* 1973, 50p.
where it may act as a spur to learning, but the accompanying drawings are unexciting and the letter-forms not always absolutely clear.

Perhaps the most successful use of transparencies is in books like :

(178) **The Magic Riddle Book** designed by Paul Taylor and illustrated by Gwen Gordon and Dave Chambers *Schlesinger* 1969, o.p.
with its joke content and its precise but gaudy pictures.

Scratch and Sniff

(179) **The Enchanted Island** designed and written by Desmond Marwood, illustrated by Richard Hook *Young World Productions:* A 'Scratch-and-Sniff Book' 1971, 65p.
The odours emitted from these 'fragrance pictures' (which, it is good to know, are 'non-toxic') are perfectly matched by the text and the illustrations.

Mirrors

(180) **Make a Bigger Puddle, Make a Smaller Worm** devised and illustrated by Marion Walter *André Deutsch* 1971, 90p.
A very ingenious play-book, which not only offers a variety of little visual experiments but also supplies a text and a group of pictures free from commercial banality.

Cut Pages

(181) **The Very Hungry Caterpillar** by Eric Carle *Hamish Hamilton* 1970, £1·25. (NY, *World* 1969).
Days of the week, fruit of the seasons, the life-cycle of a caterpillar are compounded into a story satisfying in its own right. The addition of the 'play' elements – the changing page sizes, the creature's visible and pokable tunnelings – clinch the appeal.

Other attempts to use the device of making holes in pages – in :

(182) **The Red Ladder or up, over, round and through** by Wilfried Blecher *Dent* 1973, £1·50. (Hamburg, *Gerhard Stalling*, 1972).
and :
(183) **The Secret Birthday Message** by Eric Carle *Hamish Hamilton* 1972, £1·25. (NY, *Crowell* 1971).
have worked less well because their stories have had none of the naturalness of 'the caterpillar book', although something of an exception should be made of a much earlier example of the *genre:*

(184) **The Book About Moomin, Mymble and Little My** by Tove Jansson *Benn* 1953, o.p.
Here the author's own playful spirit makes a game of the cut-outs at the same time as it confirms the book as altogether part of the more formal 'Moomin' canon.

Comparisons from the Past

Such was the inventiveness of nineteenth-century publishers and their delight in trying out new ideas that a whole exhibition could be devised based on thier play-books and book-games, for fuller discussion of which see P. Muir *English Children's Books* (Bibliograhy item 16) and Linda Hannas, *The English Jigsaw Puzzle*, 1972. The following are a few random examples:

(185) **Picture Riddles** or new nuts to crack. *Darton & Co.* n.d. [c.1860].
A group of very gnomic riddles, the easiest of which is shown here. The approach hardly compares with that of item 178.

Cinderella. Four portraits of the ugly sisters.

Item 215

Item 214

One day the King's son was to give a grand Ball. Many guests were invited but not Cinderella. She kindly helped the ugly sisters to dress for the Ball. "I wish I could go too", she pleaded. "Of course you can't", snapped the sisters.

Item 212

Item 217

Cinderella was called upon to help and advise them, for she had excellent taste. She arranged their hair most expertly, even though they cruelly teased her.

asking if she would not like to go to the balls, and saying how everyone would laugh to see a Cinderwench among the fine ladies.

Item 240

Item 242

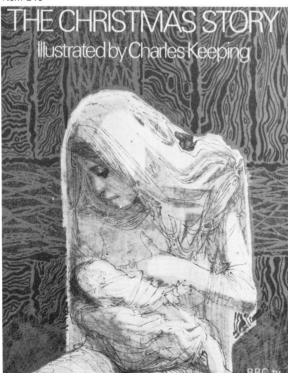

Item 245

Item 241

Mother and child. Four versions of the Nativity.

Edward Lear

and other poems

pictures by Gerald Rose

FABER AND FABER

The Dong with a Luminous Nose

Item 315

THE DONG WITH A LUMINOUS NOSE.

WHEN awful darkness and silence reign
   Over the great Gromboolian plain,
      Through the long, long wintry nights;—
   When the angry breakers roar
   As they beat on the rocky shore;—
      When Storm-clouds brood on the towering
         heights
   Of the Hills of the Chankly Bore:—

Then, through the vast and gloomy dark,
   There moves what seems a fiery spark,
   A lonely spark with silvery rays

190

Item 21

Item 316

Item 318

The Dong. Edward Lear's drawing of his Dong with a Luminous Nose, and re-creations of the character by Leslie Brook, Gerald Rose and Edward Gorey.

der the green leaves; and she let them do this as much as they liked, because green is so good for the eyes.

"Oh, how big the world is!" said the ducklings. And they certainly had much more room now than when they were lying in the egg.

"Do you suppose this is the whole world?" said their mother. "Why, it goes a long way past the other side of the garden, right into the parson's field; but I've never been as far as that. Well, you're all out now, I hope"—and she got up from her nest— "no, not all; the largest egg is still here. How ever long will it be? I can't bother about it much more." And she went on sitting again.

"Well, how's it going?" asked an old duck who came to pay a call.

8

Item 221

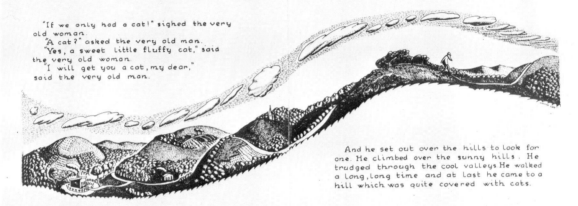

"If we only had a cat!" sighed the very old woman.
"A cat?" asked the very old man.
"Yes, a sweet little fluffy cat," said the very old woman.
"I will get you a cat, my dear," said the very old man.

And he set out over the hills to look for one. He climbed over the sunny hills. He trudged through the cool valleys. He walked a long, long time and at last he came to a hill which was quite covered with cats.

Item 265

Then the emperor tied one end of the thick strand to the heavy iron bar across the window, and the other end stretched all the way down to Djeow Seow's tiny hands.

The emperor stepped to the window sill, slipped under the iron bar, saluted the gods, and slid down the rope. His robes billowed out around him like the wings of a bright kite.

Item 231

Movement across the page. Two examples of a brilliantly dynamic use of the double-page spread, contrasted with a book that provides only a static pictorial accompaniment. (In the example shown the picture refers to text appearing three pages previously).

(186) **Little Red Riding Hood** *Dean & Son*. n.d. [?1863]
Dean's New Scenic Books, No. 1.
The text simply provides a footing for the scenery.

(187) **Letters 1 and 2** by Catherine Sinclair. Edinburgh,
James Wood, 1862.
The 'hieroglyphic' game 'warranted to keep the noisiest
child quiet for half an hour'. (See also item **257**).

(188) **All Aboard** by M. Andrews. *Ernest Nister*. n.d.
[c.1890].
A book of no distinction at all, but selling on the strength of
its shaped cover and pages.

(189) **The Fairies Playtime** with verses by Clifton
Bingham. Pen and ink illustrations by E. Stuart Hardy.
Ernest Nister. n.d. [1899].
By pulling a tab the central card wheel is made to revolve
and one fairy-tale picture dissolves into another. As can be
seen the linkings of the stories are tenuous in the extreme.
Note too the curious contrast between the art-nouveau
borders to the pictures and the Biedermeier pseudo-realism
of the pictures themselves.

(190) **Das Zauberboot** by Tom Seidmann-Freud. Berlin,
Herbert Stuffer, 1929.
A variety of play ideas are developed in this book which
differs from all the above examples in being designed for
education as much as entertainment.

(191) **Heads Bodies and Legs** by Denis Wirth-Miller and
Richard Chopping. *Penguin, Baby Puffin Books,* 1946.
A little known play-book issued in a Penguin series. At
about this time Penguin also experimented with a series of
cut-out books which included a toy theatre and Emmett's
Festival Railway.

(192) **Goldilocks and the Three Bears** illustrated by
Patricia Turner. *Folding Books Ltd*. n.d. [? 1947].
A revolving stage of pop-up scenes with a slightly coy
abridgement of the traditional tale.

10. STORIES WITHOUT WORDS

For a book like *Paddy Pork* which opens this section we find
the application of a play technique to the telling of a story
entirely in pictures. As such it may be seen legitimately as an
'alternative book', but it is also representative of a genre
which has found some favour in recent years : the picture
story without words.

These books differ from the simple, text-less object books
of Section 1 in that they make demands on the child's
ability to connect each picture with its predecessor and to
'get' the continuity and the final point through sight alone.
For this reason the books have been defended as a stimulus
to the child's pictorial sense – and, in so far as they may be
looked at with an attendant adult, they have also been seen
as occasions for the child to develop his own narrative and
conversational powers : telling the story himself, or talking
about events taking place in the illustrations. It is therefore
of prime importance that the connections between one
picture and the next, and one page and its turnover, should
be clear – in the way that they can scarcely help being in
Paddy Pork or in the comic-style progression of frames in
Father Christmas (204), where the conversation bubbles do
however provide a modicum of comment if not of narrative.

(193) **The Ballooning Adventures of Paddy Pork** by
John S. Goodall *Macmillan* 1969, 45p.
A simple, mechanical idea happily worked out in an equally
simple style. Mr Goodall's use of monochrome is so
self-sufficient that it makes the colour in the pastiche
animal drawing of a later book,
(194) **Shrewbettina's Birthday** *Macmillan* 1970, 75p.
seem superfluous.

(195) **Johnny's Bad Day** by Edward Ardizzone *Bodley
Head* 1970, 60p. (NY, *Doubleday* 1970).
Equally disarming in the simplicity of its story line and
sentiment. The way in which the story proceeds through the
pages however, and its continuity from one page opening
to the next is managed with predictable assurance.

(196) **Changes, Changes** by Pat Hutchins *Bodley Head*
1971, £1·00. (NY, *Macmillan* 1971).
A highly ingenious working out on paper of the
possibilities inherent in a collection of wooden bricks. The
urge to test the validity of all the 'changes' makes one wish
that a box of bricks might be sold along with the book.

(197) **The Knitted Cat** by Antonella Bolliger-Savelli
Hamish Hamilton 1972, £1·10. (Zürich, *Benziger* 1971).
A book whose suave professionalism belies its complete
lack of substance. Not only very little happens, but it
happens in a most confusing way and it is not only children
who will be unable to work out the purpose of the exercise.

(198) **Hide and Seek** by Renate Meyer *Bodley Head*
1969, 90p.
A book with as sketchy a story line as the foregoing, but, in
this case, intentionally so. It would seem to be the artist's
wish not so much to portray a game of hide-and-seek as to
catch the spirit of the game (just as in 53, she sought to
mirror the child's emotional involvment in playing mums
and dads). The result is a book where, despite some almost
wantonly perverse perspectives, (eg : pp. 14-15), the
atmosphere is all, and where the appeal is most directly to
someone who can draw from the pictures the atmosphere
of the game.

(199) **I See a Song** by Eric Carle *Hamish Hamilton* 1973,
£1·40. (NY, *Crowell* 1973).
A series of 'pictures' not only without words but also
without delicacy, formal attractiveness or narrative direction.
It is difficult to believe that this book is the work of the same
talent that produced *The Very Hungry Caterpillar* (181).

(200) **The Circus** by Brian Wildsmith *Oxford University
Press* 1970, £1·10.
The introductory and concluding words here serve only to
define the book's purpose as simply a procession of
descriptive paintings. As such it may be a colourful spectacle
but one devoid of any cumulative impetus and one which, in
the context of the artist's whole body of work, amounts to
little more than a repetition of known mannerisms. Contrast
it with :
(201) **Dr Anno's Magical Midnight Circus** by
Mitsumasa Anno *Weatherill* distributed in UK by *Phaidon*
1972, £1·25. (Tokyo, *Fukuinkan Shoten* 1971).
where there is a similar lack of continuity, coupled with a
certain obscurity of purpose, but where each picture at least
offers a more full-blooded story content.

"Will you take me with you?" said the dog.

"Yes," said Mr Gumpy.
"But don't tease the cat."

Item 121

THE MILK MAID

Where are you going to, my pretty maid?
I'm going a-milking, sir, she said,
Sir, she said, sir, she said,
I'm going a-milking, sir, she said.

May I go with you, my pretty maid?
You're kindly welcome, sir, she said,
Sir, she said, sir, she said,
You're kindly welcome, sir, she said.

Say, will you marry me, my pretty maid?
Yes, if you please, kind sir, she said,
Sir, she said, sir, she said,
Yes, if you please, kind sir, she said.

What is your father, my pretty maid?
My father's a farmer, sir, she said,
Sir, she said, sir, she said,
My father's a farmer, sir, she said.

What is your fortune, my pretty maid?
My face is my fortune, sir, she said,
Sir, she said, sir, she said,
My face is my fortune, sir, she said.

Then I can't marry you, my pretty maid.
Nobody asked you, sir, she said,
Sir, she said, sir, she said,
Nobody asked you, sir, she said.

THE OLD WOMAN

Old woman, old woman,
  Shall we go a-shearing?
Speak a little louder, sir,
  I'm very thick of hearing.
Old woman, old woman,
  Shall I love you dearly?
Thank you very kindly, sir,
  Now I hear you clearly.

A SAD SONG

Trip upon trenchers, and dance upon dishes,
My mother sent me for some barm, some barm;
She bid me tread lightly, and come again quickly
For fear the young men should do me some harm.
  Yet didn't you see, yet didn't you see,
  What naughty tricks they put upon me:
    They broke my pitcher,
    And spilt the water,
    And huffed my mother,
    And chid her daughter,
And kissed my sister instead of me.

BAGPIPES

Puss came dancing out of a barn
With a pair of bagpipes under her arm;
She could sing nothing but, Fiddle cum fee,
The mouse has married the humble-bee.
Pipe, cat – dance, mouse –
We'll have a wedding at our good house.

Item 75

Balance of text and picture (1). Two page openings from nursery rhyme books, printed monochrome, contrasting Raymond Briggs's scratchy and muddled use of his space with Harold Jones's delicate and finely composed frame of pictures.

Very soon they met an ice-cream man.
And the Elephant said to the Bad Baby, "Would you like an ice-cream?"
And the Bad Baby said, "Yes."
   So the Elephant stretched out his trunk and took an ice-cream for himself and an ice-cream for the Bad Baby, and they went rumpeta, rumpeta, rumpeta, all down the road, with the ice-cream man running after.

Item 120

Ladybird, ladybird, fly away home;
   Your house is on fire, your children are gone
All but one, and her name is Ann,
   And she crept under the frying-pan.

I had a little pony,
   His name was Dapple-grey;
I lent him to a lady,
   To ride a mile away.
She whipped him and she slashed him,
   She rode him through the mire;
I would not lend my pony now
   For all that lady's hire.

Leg over leg,
   As the dog went to Dover,
When he came to a stile,
   Jump he went over.

Little Robin Redbreast sat upon a tree;
Up went pussy-cat, down flew he;
Down came pussycat, away Robin ran;
Said little Robin Redbreast, Catch me if you can.
Little Robin Redbreast jumped upon a wall,
Pussy cat jumped after him, and almost had a fall,
Little Robin chirped and sang, What did pussy say?
Pussy said Meow, and Robin flew away.

82   83

Item 71

Balance of text and pictures (2). John Burningham and Raymond Briggs combining monochrome and colour in illustrations that fill out the possibilities of the text.

Item 204

↑ Item 335   ↓ Item 78

Somersault & Pepper-upper
Simmer down & eat your supper,

Artichokes & Mustard Pickle
Two for a dime or six for a nickel.

6

7

Strip cartoons. Three different treatments of narrative picture sequences.

Brian Wildsmith's *The Circus* has been followed by a similar book from the same publisher:

(202) **Joe at the Fair** by Doreen Roberts *Oxford University Press* 1972, £1·25.
The attempt to gain atmosphere resembles to some extent that in *Hide and Seek* (198) but it has none of that book's intensity of vision.

(203) **How Santa Claus Had a Long and Difficult Journey Delivering his Presents** by Fernando Krahn *Longman Young Books* 1971, £1·25. (NY, *Delacorte* 1970).
A superlative vindication of the use of near minimum resources to achieve maximum effect. The simplicity of Krahn's graphic style and his restraint in the use of colour not only enable him to get on with drawing his story without unnecessary distractions but also themselves contribute to the warmth and friendliness which make this a perfect Christmas book. Even the green backing to each page plays a part — not as a colourful indulgence but as a means of spacing the stages of the action so that each carries its full weight. In the paperback edition (*Penguin: Puffin* 1973) these green pages have been dispensed with, and the rhythm and impact of the sequence of drawings is so much the less.

In another festive picture book:

(204) **Father Christmas** by Raymond Briggs *Hamish Hamilton* 1973, £1·10.
the simple sequences of the strip-cartoon have been adopted, with conversation bubbles helping to reinforce the artist's impression of his hero as 'a type of the (not very long-suffering) common man'. Where Fernando Krahn is brief and dramatically satisfying, Raymond Briggs is extensive and rich in pictorial detail. Even so, the same warmth animates both books and, while nothing in Briggs can equal Krahn's bear and Krahn's pauky angels, the sense of Christmas excitement is entirely authentic.

11. TRADITIONAL STORIES

As with nursery rhymes, traditional tales are essentially an oral art-form. They were told before ever they were printed and they carry within themselves all the illustration that they need. Nevertheless, the universal popularity of their titles (whoever has not heard of Cinderella or Jack-the-Giant-Killer, even if they do not know the story?) made them a natural choice for every generation of children's book publishers.

Given therefore a text of best-selling potential, it is only a short step to arguing that illustration, preferably in colour, will necessarily improve the book's prospects with the public; and from that point it is only another step to arguing that modifications to the text in the interests of the illustration are entirely justified — a chain of reasoning which has resulted in the serious distortion of many fine tales. There are of course other contributory reasons for distortion: in particular the weak or inaccurate translation of foreign stories (especially Grimm or Andersen) and the bowdlerisation of incidents in the supposed interest of the child of tender sensibility.

Quite apart from the textual modifications that may occur in picture book versions of traditional tales, there is also a serious danger that insensitive illustration will damage the child's imaginative response to a primarily oral narrative. One of the classic examples of this is demonstrated here in *The Tinder Box* (218-9) where little artists have come to grief over Andersen's big dogs; but injury can also be done to the total atmosphere of a story by the selection of inappropriate graphic styles. The clue to success perhaps lies in the recognition that the self-effacing quality of the best traditional book illustration — its tendency to give priority to the story rather than to special graphic effects — is highly suitable for popular tales.

11a COLLECTIONS

Some idea of the norms from which illustrators depart at their peril is given in such nineteenth century collections, now reprinted, as:

(205) **English Fairy Tales** collected by Joseph Jacobs, illustrated by John D. Batten (*Alfred Nutt* 1890). NY, *Dover* 1967 £1·00 distributed in UK by *Constable;* and

(206) **More English Fairy Tales** collected by Joseph Jacobs, illustrated by John D. Batten (*Alfred Nutt* 1894), NY *Dover* 1967, £1·00.

(207) **Perrault's Fairy Tales,** illustrated by Gustave Doré illustrations 1867, Dover edition 1969, £1·00.
Vastly different in style though they be, both are ultimately rooted in the tradition that demands of an illustrator that his work harmonise with his story. John D. Batten may achieve this by a multitude of simple details, Gustave Doré by a sweep of romantic visualisation (certainly much closer in scale and format to the contemporary picture book), yet each is true to the spirit of the text.

In terms of the modern book, something of their style, though not necessarily influence, may be seen in, say:

(208) **Tales from Grimm** freely translated and illustrated by Wanda Gág *Faber* 1937, £1·70. (NY, *Coward* 1936).

or in Robin Jacques's illustrations for the many story collections by Ruth Manning-Sanders, stories from which appear in:

(209) **A Choice of Magic** by Ruth Manning-Sanders *Methuen* 1971, £2·00.

Given such care for a true reflection of the oral art of fairy-tale, it is mournful that a mutilation of that art can achieve the popularity of:

(210) **Walt Disney's Giant Book of Fairy Tales** *Purnell* 1972, £1·75.
whose sentimental text and 'wonderful full colour illustrations' may, for many children, come to be the definitive images of some of our most powerful fairy stories.

Indeed one does not really need Walt Disney to emphasise so comprehensively the dangers of colour pictures 'taking over' the duties of the text. Even a collection with the credentials of:

(211) **The Fairy Tale Treasury,** selected by Virginia Haviland and illustrated by Raymond Briggs *Hamish Hamilton* 1972, £3·00.

tends to set more store by illustrative gimmicks than by establishing and preserving a consistent and sympathetic view of the tales.

11b. SINGLE TALES

Because of their bulk, most fairy-tale collections (including some noted above) are hardly eligible for consideration as picture books. Critical attention here must focus on the conversion to picture books of single tales, which are usually portioned out to make up a volume of thirty-two pages. Under these circumstances, it is natural that the illustrations will tend to assume a dominant role and the following examples (from a truly multitudinous number of versions in print) have been chosen to show some of the best and worst that is being done.

i) CINDERELLA

The following editions of Perrault's famous tale form something of a summary of the ways in which a single tale may be treated, almost none of them achieving a satisfactory reconciliation of the realistic and Romantic elements in the story :

(212) **Cinderella** A *Sandle* Book n.d. o.p.
Bought recently for 3p, this production – almost anonymous as to publisher as well as author and artist – shows at its crudest the conventional Cinderella of the newsagent's counter. The text does at least have a certain briskness about it which is rather more commendable than that of :

(213) **Cinderella** by Vera Southgate. Illustrated by Eric Winter *Ladybird* 1964, 15p.
where a refinement of the conventional illustrations (why does Cinderella never look filthy ?) is accompanied by an altogether more ponderous text. The well-meaning attempt to turn the story into a supplementary reader for a reading scheme has resulted in a strange mixing of flat modern statements and quasi-poetic 'traditional' phrasing.

(214) **Cinderella** drawn by Dick Bruna *Methuen* 1968, 45p. (Utrecht, *A. W. Bruna & Zoon* 1966).
This is in many ways the oddest of the examples given here, since it shows the application of Bruna's well-known style to a narrative for which it is, by its very nature, unsuited. Adults who know the story will, however, get considerable entertainment out of observing Mr Bruna's expressive delineations of his characters' mouths.

(215) **Cinderella** or the little glass slipper by Charles Perrault illustrated by Errol Le Cain *Faber* 1972, £1·25.
A *tour de force* in the Romantic style, after which one feels that the illustrators of items 212 and 213 were striving. Mr Le Cain's brilliant decorations are however at once too splendid and too clever to suit Perrault's simple tale (whose text has been used as a basis for this rewritten version).

(216) **Cinderella** retold in story and collage by Alan Suddon, with a French translation by Claude Aubry *Dobson* 1969, £1·50. (Ottawa, *Oberon Press*, 1969).
A version which, with its bicycles and electric kettles, is presumably intended as a bit of a joke. The publisher's dust jacket draws attention to Mr Suddon's 'breath-taking collages . . . reproduced with the utmost purity and perfection' and remarks that the 'brilliant, witty, joyous and comic' text is 'for today's child'. *Caveat emptor.*

(217) **Cinderella** or the little glass slipper by Charles Perrault, illustrated by Shirley Hughes *Bodley Head* 1970, 90p.
Given the need to convert a story into a picture book, this unassuming version at least has the twin virtues of a text close to Perrault's own, and a set of illustrations which, by their very matter-of-factness, set off the magical transformation at the heart of the story.

For another adaptation of the story in popular form see item 166. See also the unhappy treatment of the story at the hands of Walt Disney and Raymond Briggs, above (210 and 211).

ii) HANS CHRISTIAN ANDERSEN

A difficult author to translate as well as illustrate, and for much the same reasons. The genius of his stories lies not just in their shape and their pointedness, but also in the tone of voice of their telling, a very subtle blend of the casual, the colloquial, the ironic and the Romantic. Clumsy translation and over-emphatic illustration alike undermine or sentimentalise the nuances.

(218) **The Tinderbox** from the story by Hans Christian Andersen, with pictures by Eva Johanna Rubin *Methuen* 1967, 75p. (Berlin, *Der Kinderbuchverlag*, 1964).
A modified text with toy-town illustrations. They would certainly be suitable for coping with a 'Punch and Judy' book – as witness the charming pattern work on page 14 – but they come nowhere near the dramatic requirements of Andersen's story.

(219) **The Tinder Box** adapted from the story by Hans Christian Andersen, illustrated by Brychta *Watts* 1972, 80p.
The 'adaptation' takes the story in the direction of flat gossip ; the pictures are unable to hit upon a uniform approach or style – sometimes bled to the edge, sometimes framed, sometimes comic in a sub-Ungerer way, sometimes merely scenic. The treatment of the famous dogs reduces the awesome to the merely ludicrous.

(220) **The Ugly Duckling** by Hans Christian Andersen, illustrated by Johannes Larsen *Kaye & Ward* 1971, 95p.
Not so much illustrations as a sequence of paintings – true enough in their atmosphere – to go with the story. No attempt is made to integrate them with the text, some in fact appearing as much as two leaves out of phase.

(221) **The Ugly Duckling.** Story for pictures by Charlotte Kindray, pictures by Osamu Isukasu *Hamlyn* 1967, o.p.
A fine example of the featureless style of the 'international colour book' made to be marketed anywhere in the world, appropriate words in appropriate languages being overprinted on the tame and inoffensive colour pictures. It will be noticed that, in the course of universalisation, the original author's name has disappeared entirely.

(222) **The Nightingale** by Hans Christian Andersen, illustrated by Kaj Beckman *Kaye & Ward* 1972, £1·10. (NY, *Van Nostrand* 1972).
Perhaps the peak of all Andersen's achievements – a story so subtle in its tones as really to be unillustrable. Certainly this series of paintings which, like those for *The Ugly Duckling* (220 above), serve merely as scene settings, nowhere approximates to the story's strange moods of satire and nostalgia.

(223) **The Nightingale** by Hans Christian Andersen, designed and illustrated by Nancy Ekholm Burkert *Collins* 1967, £1·05. (NY, *Harper* 1965).
A boldly original attempt to overcome some of the difficulties of the illustrator's task, by adopting a mixture of pastiche styles : *chinoiserie* and *art nouveau*. Mrs Burkert's technical skill in the huge spread pictures is very compelling and her marginal drawings in monochrome strike a fine balance between illustration and decoration. It is difficult to see how, given the wish to convert the story into a picture book, such a solution could be bettered.

(224) **The Steadfast Tin Soldier** by Hans Christian Andersen, with pictures by Monika Laimgruber *Hamish Hamilton* 1970, £1·25. (Zürich, *Atlantis* 1970).
Another attempt to match technique with technique. Like *The Nightingale*, this story offers the illustrator a profoundly difficult task, and one which has evoked from Mrs Laimgruber a brilliant display of her powers (even though her use of dotted shading suggests that everything is affected by woodworm). By concentrating on a few scenes, lavishing upon them a wealth of detailed colour composition, she is able to convince the reader that this indeed was how it all happened.

iii) VARIA

A miscellany of examples that may help to suggest directions or point up contrasts :

(225) **The Old Woman and her Pig** pictures by Paul Galdone *Bodley Head* 1961, £1·15. (NY, *McGraw-Hill* 1960).
A further application of Paul Galdone's unpretentious narrative style to a story that needs nothing more ornate (see also items 91 and 93 above). How easy it is to overdo the treatment of a cumulative tale of this kind can be seen in :

(226) **One Fine Day** by Nonny Hogrogian *Hamish Hamilton* 1972, £1·40. (NY, *Macmillan* 1971).
an altogether smoother product, but one whose text lacks the compulsive rhythm of *The Old Woman* and whose pictures for all their pleasant use of colour are perfunctory in their attempts to match the content of the story.

(227) **Drummer Hoff** adapted by Barbara Emberley, illustrated by Ed Emberley *Bodley Head* 1970, 90p. (NY, *Prentice-Hall*, 1967).
A fine example of how a series of pictures planned very much as two-dimensional patterns can, by virtue of wit and the intelligent control of line and colour, measure up to the demands of a traditional cumulative rhyme.

(228) **The Great Big Enormous Turnip** by Alexei Tolstoy, pictures by Helen Oxenbury *Heinemann* 1968, £1·00.
An equally successful application of a more discursive, 'realistic' style, which may be compared to the Russian interpretation of the 1930's at item 369.

(229) **The Extraordinary Tug of War,** retold by Letta Schatz, illustrated by John Burningham *Bodley Head* 1969, 90p. (Chicago, *Follett*, 1968).
The text of this Nigerian tale has been prepared very much as a virtuoso piece for storytellers, but John Burningham has met virtuosity with virtuosity in establishing a comic

style for his illustrations and in sustaining it over the unusual distance of forty-eight pages. The book contrasts strongly with :

(230) **Anansi the Spider** adapted and illustrated by Gerald McDermott *Hamish Hamilton* 1973, £1·40. (NY, *Holt* 1972).
a tale from neighbouring Ghana, which replaces Letta Schatz's slightly overwritten text with a colloquial telling of extreme brevity, and which uses a symbolic series of illustrations drawn from the woven designs of Ashanti fabrics. Reading the pictures now becomes less the enjoyment of narrative scenes than the working out of diagrammatic puzzles.

Two other examples of picture books seeking to catch the flavour of a national illustrative style are :

(231) **The Emperor and the Kite** by Jane Yolen, pictures by Ed Young *Macdonald* 1969, o.p.
with its restrained but enormously effective use of double-page spreads ; and :

(232) **The Woodcutter's Duck** by Krystyna Turska *Hamish Hamilton* 1972, £1·40.
with its reference in figure groupings and page design to the traditions of European folk art.

(233) **The Sleeping Beauty** by the Grimm brothers, illustrated by F. Hoffmann *Oxford University Press* 1959, £1·15.
Limitations of space have prevented the tales of Grimm from receiving even so brief a note as those of Hans Christian Andersen — albeit there are as many travesties of the one in picture book form as there are of the other. Hence this one edition of one tale must stand as exemplary both in its respect for the text of the story and in the Romantic play of its beautifully composed pictures.

(234) **The Babes in the Wood,** illustrated by Edward Ardizzone *Bodley Head* 1972, £1·00.
(235) **Jack the Giant-Killer** from the version by Joseph Jacobs, illustrated by Fritz Wegner *Bodley Head* 1970, 90p.
Two English folk-tales illustrated with responsive sympathy and included here for comparison with the nineteenth century versions at 255 and 256.

iv) BIBLE STORIES

As with folk-tale, so with scripture — our image of certain heroes and events may be fixed almost for life through the pictures that are set before us in childhood. There is little room here to examine as it deserves to be examined the history of cliche in religious illustration, but the following few examples note the norms and some attempts to escape from them :

(236) **The Shepherd Boy of Bethlehem** by Lucy Diamond with illustrations by Kenneth Inns. *Ladybird* 1953, 15p.
A re-told version with typical 'Sunday School' illustrations — David as spick and span throughout his adventures as Cinderella (213) was through hers.

(237) **David and Goliath,** illustrated by Alan Howard *Faber* 1970, £1·00.
The text now being that of the Authorised Version, slightly edited — the strength of the words inspiring the illustrator to an interpretation which is not only dramatic but comic as well — a rare event in Bible stories.

(238) **The Story of Jonah, being the whole book of Jonah** illustrated by Barry Wilkinson *Bodley Head:* A Bodley Head Bible Picture Book 1968, o.p.
An even more thoroughgoing use of the text of the Authorised Version, adopted for all the volumes of this series. Once again it has moved the illustrator towards seeking to reflect the truth of the story, rather than merely trying to produce a sort of theological Sinbad the Sailor.

(239) **Jonah and the Lord** by George Macbeth, pictures by Margaret Gordon *Macmillan* 1969, 90p.
A very strange telling of the tale whose printed lines perversely move against the cunningly worked up verbal rhythms. Miss Gordon's faintly medieval pictures do not have quite the same dramatic feeling as Barry Wilkinson's, their heavy structure suggesting that the whole thing is a celestial joke.

(240) **The Little Lord Jesus** by Lucy Diamond, with illustrations by Kenneth Inns *Ladybird* 1954, 15p.
First of a group of picture books about the Nativity which, even if stripped of its theological significance or its sentimental associations, remains an event that lives in the imagination. How far the story's strength lies in the measured dignity of the Authorised Version cannot here be assessed and I have largely avoided detailed comment on the quality of the retellings. Surely, though, in visual terms, the Nativity is not an event to be pictured in the trite terms of the little volume noted above nor with the chocolate-box painting of :

(241) **The Christmas Story** retold by Elizabeth David *Ward Lock* 1972.
No illustrator is named for this book, the pictures being credited to the Augsburg Publishing House, Minneapolis.

(242) **The Christmas Story** illustrated by Reinhard Herrmann *Macmillan* 1962, 90p. (Gütersloh, *Gert Mohn* 1962).
is at least unpretentious in its naïveté, even though the mannered simplifications rob the story of all its mystery.

(243) **The Holy Night** with illustrations by Celestino Piatti *Bodley Head* 1968, £1·05. (Zürich, *Artemis* 1968).
which uses the text of St Luke's Gospel, has a greater visual warmth but specialises in giving everyone an electric glare behind the eyes, which is very distracting.

(244) **Long Ago in Bethlehem** by Masahiro Kasuya *Black* 1973, £1·25. (Tokyo, *Shiko-Sha* 1972).
A Japanese version, with a text bordering on the sentimental and a series of paintings which escape the same accusation by placing their subjects behind a lithographic mist.

(245) **The Christmas Story** : as told on Play School, illustrated by Charles Keeping *BBC* 1968, 70p.
Although first conceived as a series of stills for a television programme, this brings into book form what is surely the truest interpretation yet. The simple text allows full play to

Charles Keeping's decorations which, with their muted colours and their expressive line, dispel all sentimental implications and reach towards the heart of the story.

Comparisons from the Past

(246) 'Cinderella ; or The Little Glass Slipper' in **Histories or Tales of Past Times.** Told by Mother Goose. *Fortune Press* n.d. [?1935].
The wood-cut head-piece, that appeared in many variant cuttings as the only illustration of the story in its earliest editions. Printed from a woodcut made by Victor Stuyvaert from a photograph of the cuts in 'the twelfth edition, dated 1802'.

(247) **The Curious Adventures of the Beautiful Little Maid Cinderilla** : or the history of a glass slipper. Colchester, *I. Marsden* n.d. [c.1815]
A crude woodcut of the ugly sisters in a penny chapbook edition.

(248) **The Children's Nursery Picture Book of Favourite Stories** Edinburgh, *Gall & Inglis*. n.d. [c.1870].
A double-page spread of the Cinderella story in this Victorian collection.

(249) **Cinderella** *George Routledge & Sons* n.d. [1873].
Another example of Walter Crane's elaborate art.

(250) **Cinderella** *Frederick Warne & Co.* n.d. [?1910].
(The Wonder Toys, second series).
A cheap edition which shares the intention of our contemporary one noted at 212 above. The back cover is an advertisement for Pears Soap.

(251) **Het Lelijke Jonge Eendje** . . . van Hans Christian Andersen, illustrated by Theo Van Hoytema. Laren, *Schoonderbeek* 1970).
Facsimile of a famous Dutch edition of 'The Ugly Duckling' first published in 1893 with lithographed illustrations which exhibit a powerful control of page design.

(252) **Hans Andersen's Fairy Tales** selected and edited for little folk. Illustrated by Helen Stratton. *Blackie*, 1904.
A rather more confident treatment of the three dogs than is shown in our modern examples.

(253) **Tri Medvedya** by Count Lev Nicolaevich Tolstoi, Leningrad 1935.
A Russian edition of 'The Three Bears' which serves also as an example of the new use of colour lithography in the mass-production of children's books which occurred in the 1930's. See item 369 below.

(254) **The Sleeping Beauty** *George Routledge & Sons.* n.d. [1876]. (Walter Crane's Toy Books No. 116).
Crane at his most heavily ornamental. The rhymed version of the story almost disappears into the undergrowth.

(255) **Jack the Giant-Killer** by Richard Doyle. *Eyre & Spottiswoode*. n.d. [1888].
Reproduction of a manuscript version of the story which Doyle made in 1842 at the age of eighteen, included with the following example of Randolph Caldecott in sombre mood :

(256) **The Babes in the Wood** *George Routledge & Sons.*
n.d. [1879]. (R. Caldecott's Picture Books).
For comparison with items 235 and 234 above.

(257) **The Modern Hieroglyphical Bible** designed to
promote the amusement and instruction of youth. *R. Harrild*
1815.
Pictures converting Bible reading into something of a game.
The solutions to the not very difficult puzzles appear at the
bottom of the page.

(258) **Bible Pictures and Stories** New Testament. *SPCK*
n.d. [c.1870].
A coloured book for Sunday School use.

(259) **The Childhood of Christ** *Frederick Warne* n.d.
[1872] (Aunt Louisa's Sunday Books)
A heavy Victorian interpretation in 'classical' style. The
illustration shown is signed Moyr Smith.

12. THE NOVEL IN PICTURES

Because of their tendency to be large in format and slim in
girth ('flats' as the merchandisers like to call them), picture
story-books are often lumped together as an homogeneous
unit. Enough has already been said to show that this is an
over-simplified view, and the purpose of the present section
is to show how longer stories or stories with more complex
ideas have been accommodated in picture books.

It is obvious that the books considered here have a close
relationship to the simple picture books discussed in
Section 7 and, indeed, no clear line of division may be
drawn between them. On the whole though the present
array of books is characterised by a greater insistence upon
'story' as opposed to 'incident' than in the previous section
and a disappearance of the cumulations and repetitions
which relate the simpler books to the simpler folk tales.

Even so, the criteria for judging the success of these books
are much the same as those applied in Section 7. A more
extended story is not an excuse for slack or verbose texts,
and one of the key demands that is made upon illustrators
working in this field is the need to pace story and picture
uniformly through the book so that the one is constantly
related to and working with the other. This will call for the
same flexible use of pages and a like degree of balance
between text and illustration. Longer stories may also,
however, raise more sharply the question of illustrative
content. So the words of a story come to do more and more
work, so the illustrator's responsibility changes and it
becomes necessary for him to decide how far he is simply
reflecting the tale in pictures, how far adding to it further
visual details and how far creating for it an atmosphere, a
sense of local habitation, without which it would be
lacking a dimension.

The number of books eligible for inclusion in this category is
so huge that endless permutations could have been devised
for demonstrating a variety of critical approaches. It would
for instance have been possible to show how a worthy
moral story, worthily illustrated, like :

(260) **The Emir's Son** by Martin Ballard, illustrated by
Gareth Floyd *Longman* 1967, o.p.
fails because it is too heavily weighted in its text to make a
satisfactory picture book ; or how a fantasy upon which
every care of designer and printer has been lavished, like :

(261) **Gold Steps Stone Steps** by Paul Margulies,
illustrated by J. K. Lambert *Harlin Quist* 1970, £1·05,
distributed in UK by *W. H. Allen.*
fails because it is at once too frail as a story and too
sophisticated in its presentation ; or how a popular book
like :

(262) **Giants Come in Different Sizes** by Jolly Roger
Bradfield *Ward Lock* 1971, 80p.
fails (as do so many popular picture books) through crudity
and over-emphasis – a good idea spoiled by its too hasty
execution.

In the event, however, I have decided to exhibit a small
selection of picture books which show in one form or
another the tradition of children's book illustration at its best
and which may serve as a broad criterion against which
other books in the genre may be measured. No attempt has
been made to present more than a selection of styles and
manners of approach and the notes are confined to pointing
out the chief reason for the book's inclusion. Certain books
that call for special critical consideration have been put
forward in a group of sub-sections at the end.

(263) **The Story of the Little Red Engine** by Diana Ross,
pictures by Leslie Wood *Faber* 1945, 95p.
Something of a transitional volume, since the length of the
book is the result of a highly successful use of verbal
repetitions, which make the story a classic for reading
aloud. The planning of the illustrations shows a like success,
from the link-up with the (simplified) map on the first page
through all the scenes of the story, with the 'dig a dig' motif
bringing text and graphic work into a close association.

(Historically the series of 'Little Red Engine' books is also
interesting, since their illustrative style was established not
by Leslie Wood but by the two Polish artists Jan Lewitt and
George Him, who used the composite name Lewitt-Him.
Items 293 and 294 show their *Little Red Engine Gets a
Name* and an English edition of their *Lokomotyva*, first
published in Warsaw in 1938.) See B. Hürlimann *Three
Centuries of Children's Books in Europe* (Bibliography
item 10) pp 227–8.

(264) **The Little White Hen** written by Anita Hewett and
drawn by William Stobbs *Bodley Head* 1962, 70p.
The stylised illustration of the previous example is here
carried a stage closer to simple pattern work, but again
without any interference in the progress of a story that has
all the fluency of the best of folk-tales.

(265) **Millions of Cats** by Wanda Gág *Faber* 1929, 70p.
(NY, *Coward* 1928).
Another story in the manner of folk-tale, here matched with
illustrations that owe much to the woodcuts of popular
tradition. For all its monochrome simplicity, however, there
is a fine precision in the way that the story and the pictures
work together making creative use of the advantages of a
hand-written text.

(266) **Gone is Gone** or the story of the man who wanted to do housework by Wanda Gág *Faber* 1936, 55p. (NY, *Coward* 1935).
is the retelling of a folk-tale in which both format and design further demonstrate her fine talent for adapting the illustrative style of the chapbook tradition.

(267) **The Little Wooden Farmer** by Alice Dalgliesh, illustrated by Anita Lobel *Hamish Hamilton* 1969, 90p. (NY, *Macmillan* 1968).
Where Wanda Gág shows herself a master of the simplicity of a 'folk' style, Anita Lobel shows herself master of its ornamental qualities. While her pictures throughout this little tale are a delight, it is a delight redoubled through the commentary which she has stitched into the sequence of its decorative borders.

(268) **The Cabbage Princess** by Errol Le Cain *Faber* 1969, £1·00.
In his *Cinderella* (215) Mr Le Cain was illustrating what is essentially a popular tale; here he is dealing with one of his own devising. He has therefore been able to prepare a text that is better suited to his gift for ornamentation and colour, his command of the formalities of gesture and grouping.

(269) **The Bee-man of Orn** by Frank R. Stockton, illustrated by Maurice Sendak *Collins* 1967, 80p. (NY, *Holt* 1964).
(270) **The Griffin and the Minor Canon** story by Frank R. Stockton, pictures by Maurice Sendak *Collins* 1967, 80p. (NY, *Holt* 1964).
Earlier examples of Maurice Sendak's work have been confined to his shorter picture books; here he brings his artistry to bear on two longer stories that are themselves of considerable distinction. By choosing, in each case, an illustrative style that echoes the past – in *The Bee-man* the English colour work of Rowlandson and Caldecott, in *The Griffin* the 'tighter' style of the line engravers – Maurice Sendak is able to place Frank Stockton's stories in an appropriate atmosphere. At the same time he contributes the entirely Sendakian qualities of controlled design throughout each book, and a most warm reflection of the author's own sense of humour.

(271) **Captain Slaughterboard Drops Anchor** story and drawings by Mervyn Peake *Academy Editions* n.d. [1967] 60p.
First published plain in 1939 and later, 1945, in an edition that superimposed upon the line-work a variety of flat, pastel shades, *Captain Slaughterboard's* more recent printings in black and yellow only help to emphasise how far the quality of the book lies in its drawing. The exotic, preposterous narrative and the parade of grotesques – both man and beast – are given an exact, defined reality through the detail and the at times almost fungoidal elaboration of the artist's line. It is regrettable that the full impact of Peake's work has been lessened through its reduction in size for this paperback edition. (See item 295).

(272) **The Beast of Monsieur Racine** by Tomi Ungerer *Bodley Head* 1972, £1·50. (NY, *Farrar* 1971).
Tomi Ungerer is also a master of the grotesque (most conspicuously in his cartoons, which by no means fall within the terms of reference of this exhibition). *The Beast of Monsieur Racine* shows at its best not only his delight in caricature and in scenes of conviviality or mayhem, but also his abundance of visual ideas for the composition and

decoration of his pictures. (Note especially his engagement with the possibilities of the frame for his illustrations. Note too the fraternal homage of the dedication to Maurice Sendak). Three further examples of his versatility are the early and comparatively simple:

(273) **Crictor** by Tomi Ungerer *Methuen* 1959, 80p. (NY, *Harper* n.d.)
and the more recent extravaganzas:

(274) **Zeralda's Ogre** by Tomi Ungerer *Bodley Head* 1970, £1·25. (NY, *Harper* 1967).
and:
(275) **The Sorcerer's Apprentice** by Barbara Hazen, illustrated by Tomi Ungerer *Methuen* 1971, £1·20. (Boston, *Little Brown* 1962).

(276) **I Had Trouble in Getting to Solla Sollew** by Dr Seuss *Collins* 1967, £1·00. (NY, *Random House*, 1965.)
A full development of both the narrative and the illustrative elements present in, say, *Green Eggs and Ham* (157) or *The Cat in the Hat* (154). The didactic *raison d'être* (which is a feature of many of Dr Seuss's longer stories) contrasts sharply with the strenuous farce of the ballad and its double-page illustrations, to say nothing of the procession of skritzes, skrinks, camels and other members of Dr Seuss's comic menagerie.

(277) **Orlando** (the Marmalade Cat) **Buys a Farm** by Kathleen Hale *Cape* 1942, new edition 1972, 90p.
Like some other pictures of the thirties and forties (eg: items 288 and 302), the 'Orlando' books have suffered at the hands of recent publishers. Their strength has never lain in their texts, which are often wordy and over-descriptive, but always in their richly detailed and colourful illustrations. Through a reduction of the books' page-sizes by approximately half, however, and through a loss of definition in the modern printings, much of the highly original and absorbing character of the books has now disappeared. (See item 296).

Something of the flavour is still preserved in the more happily designed:

(278) **Henrietta the Faithful Hen** by Kathleen Hale *Allen & Unwin* 1967, 75p. First published 1943.
where the modern edition has effected less drastic changes.

(279) **The Tale of Peter Rabbit** by Beatrix Potter *Warne*, 40p.
(280) **The Tale of Samuel Whiskers** by Beatrix Potter *Warne*, 40p.
(281) **The Tale of Mr Tod** by Beatrix Potter *Warne*, 40p.
As has already been implied (page 24) Beatrix Potter's stories are not uniform in anything but their present-day format and design. Both length and illustrative approach were dependent upon the requirements of the tale that had to be told and it is regrettable that, just as the panorama form of the shorter books has been abandoned, so too has the variant styling of these three books, which rank among the finest examples of Beatrix Potter's command over word and image. (Needless to say the requirements of mass-production which have led to a standardisation of format have led also to a serious decline in the standard of reproduction of the monochrome and the coloured illustrations.)

See items 299 and 300, and the account of the publication of the books given in L. Linder *History of the Writings of Beatrix Potter* (Bibliography item 57) — not least her castigation of her publisher's timidity in the matter of *Mr. Tod* (p.211).

(282) **The Little House** by Virginia Lee Burton *Faber,* 1946 £1·20. (NY, *Hougton* 1942).
A precursor of the 'pollution' stories noted on page 46, but how much more reticent in its treatment of the spread of urbanisation and how much more gripping in its portrayal of change, and in the 'character' which is bestowed upon 'the little house'. Part of Virginia Lee Burton's skill lies in the way that she catches the detail of everyday events and carries that detail forward through a series of pages — as also, for instance, in :

(283) **Mike Mulligan and his Steam Shovel** by Virginia Lee Burton *Faber* 1966, £1·10. (NY, *Hougton* 1939).

(284) **Humbert, Mr Firkin and the Lord Mayor of London** written and illustrated by John Burningham. *Cape* 1965, £1·25.
Dedicated to 'Scrap Dealers, Brewers, Coal Merchants, Lord Mayors and all who continue to use horses', this urban comedy shows the vein of spirited caricature that runs through John Burningham's picture-book tales. It contrasts amusingly with its almost exact contemporary, Charles Keeping's *Shaun and the Carthorse* (354).

(285) **The Flying Postman** by V. H. Drummond *Longman Young Books* new edition 1964. (*Penguin* and NY, *Houghton* 1948).
(286) **Meal One** by Ivor Cutler, pictures by Helen Oxenbury *Heinemann* 1971, £1·10.
(287) **A Penny to see the Pier** by Michael O'Leary, illustrated by John Haslam *Longman Young Books* 1967, 75p.
Three fantasies set in an everyday world, each of them differing in subject, tempo and illustrative style but all informed by a sense of humour that is reflected and sharpened by the pictures.

(288) **Little Tim and the Brave Sea Captain** by Edward Ardizzone *Oxford University Press* second edition 1955, £1·00.
First of the ten adventures of 'Little Tim' which have recently concluded with the publication of :

(289) **Tim's Last Voyage** by Edward Ardizzone *Bodley Head* 1973, £1·00.
All partake of Edward Ardizzone's genius in balancing the tone and colour of his text with that of his illustration so that the reader almost loses sight of how profoundly satisfying the illustrations are. (Although once again here, the reduction in size of the early volumes of the series, and the abandonment of a hand-written script have detracted slightly from the individual character which the series originally possessed.) See the accounts of the inception of 'Little Tim' in its author's *The Young Ardizzone* (Bibliography item 29) pp 144 and in *Illustrators of Children's Books 1957–1966* (Bibliography item 14).

Further examples of the way in which Edward Ardizzone is able to adapt his individual, immediately recognisable style to suit the mood of a variety of texts are :
(290) **Diana and her Rhinoceros** by Edward Ardizzone *Bodley Head* 1964, 70p.
(291) **Titus in Trouble** by James Reeves, illustrated by Edward Ardizzone *Bodley Head* 1959, 90p.
(292) **The Night Ride** by Aingelda Ardizzone, illustrated by Edward Ardizzone, *Longman Young Books*, 1973, £1·45.

Comparisons from the Past
(confined here chiefly to displaying earlier editions of the books discussed above).

(293) **Locomotive. The Turnip. The Birds' Broadcast.** Rhymes by Julian Tuwim, drawings by Lewitt and Him. *Minerva Publishing Co.* n.d. [1939].
The English edition, printed in Poland, of **Lokomotyva** [1938] and progenitor of :

(294) **The Little Red Engine Gets a Name.** Story by Diana Ross. Pictures by Lewitt-Him. *Faber* n.d. [1942].

(295) **Captain Slaughterboard Drops Anchor** by Mervyn Peake. *Country Life* 1939 ; *Eyre & Spottiswoode* 1945. Lent by Maeve Gilmore.

(296) **Orlando (The Marmalade Cat) A Trip Abroad** by Kathleen Hale. *Country Life*, 1938.

(297) **The Tale of Peter Rabbit** by Beatrix Potter *Warne* 1902.
A plate from an early edition showing the rather superior half-tone colour printing of the time, and also juxtaposed with :

(298) **Peter Rabbit** story by Beatrix Potter, pictures by Leonard Weisgard. NY, *Grosset & Dunlap*, 1955.
One of several vulgarisations which have been published in the United States, where the book failed to achieve copyright protection on its first publication.

(299) **The Roly-Poly Pudding** by Beatrix Potter. *Warne* 1908.
(300) **The Tale of Mr Tod** by Beatrix Potter. *Warne* 1912.
First editions of the books discussed under items 280-281.

(301) **Little Tim and the Brave Sea Captain** by Edward Ardizzone, London and NY, *Oxford University Press* 1936.
First edition, lithographed in America of the first of the 'Little Tim' books, showing the generous format and the hand-written script noted above at item 289.

(302) **Histoire de Babar le petit éléphant** par Jean de Brunhoff, Paris, *Hachette* 1931.
The first French edition of the first of the Babar books, showing the large format, the fine lithographic printing and the hand-written text, whose subsequent loss is discussed below.

12a. THE RAPE OF BABAR, AND SOME OTHERS

Just as Little Tim and Orlando have declined since the more spacious days of the nineteen-thirties, so too Babar the little Elephant has suffered at the hands of later generations. The original *Story of Babar* by Jean de Brunhoff was translated from the French and published by Methuen in 1934, a large folio whose pages were entirely personal to their creator, planned so that the illustrations and hand-written text should fit together as a complete unit. (See *Three Centuries of Children's Books in Europe* (Bibliography item 10) pp 194–200).

Six further volumes in the 'Babar' series were prepared by Jean de Brunhoff before his death in 1937, and in their original state these represent Babar at his best — an appealing character moving through a series of adventures that draw their quality from the relaxed storytelling and the inventive illustrations of their author. Since that time however the popularity of Babar has been exploited so that the original stories have been lost behind adaptations and the many sequels devised by Jean's son, Laurent de Brunhoff.

In demonstration of this point there are shown here:
(303) **The Story of Babar** by Jean de Brunhoff *Methuen* 1934, reprinted 1955, 80p. (Paris, *Hachette* 1931).
the original story, now reduced to almost half its original size, with the hand-lettering replaced by formal typography and with the colour printing bereft of all subtlety of colouring. Along with the rest of the modern issues of Jean de Brunhoff's books it is a poor shadow of its great predecessor.

It has however suffered even more than this, as witness:
(304) **Babar's Childhood** by Jean de Brunhoff *Methuen* 1969, 40p (Paris, *Hachette* 1951).

(305) **Babar and the Old Lady** by Jean de Brunhoff *Methuen* 1969, 40p (Paris, *Hachette* 1951).

(306) **Babar's Coronation** by Jean de Brunhoff *Methuen* 1969, 40p (Paris, *Hachette* 1952).
where the original story has been sliced into three parts and published in a book about a quarter of the size of the first edition. Both text and illustrations have been altered where the new format and the new three-part story required, and the printing both in its colour and its detail of line is even worse than in the shrunk edition of *The Story of Babar*.

For purposes of comparison the exhibition also includes:

(307) **Babar and the Professor** by Laurent de Brunhoff *Methuen* 1972, 95p. (Paris, *Hachette* 1956). (NY, *Random House* 1966).
the latest English version of Laurent de Brunhoff's many sequels to the original 'Babar' series;

(308) **Babar Loses his Crown**, a 'Babar' book in Dr Seuss's 'Beginner Books' series *Collins* 1968, 60p. (NY, *Random House* n.d.).

(309) **Babar Goes Visiting**, a photographic volume based upon the television series by Laurent de Brunhoff. *Methuen* 1969, 75p. (Paris, *Hachette* 1969).

Nor is Babar the only character to find himself altered almost out of recognition by our age's restless desire to tamper with accepted forms — even when these accepted forms are recognised as being in some respects definitive. Consider for instance the fate of Winnie-the-Pooh in such picture books as:

(310) **Pooh's Book** by A. A. Milne, adapted by Rosemary Garland *Nelson:* Reading with Winnie-the-Pooh series n.d., o.p.
and:
(311) **Winnie-the-Pooh. A Tight Squeeze.** A story by A. A. Milne *Purnell* 1973, 75p.
In the first, quite inadmissible changes are made to the original text, and in both the quiet accompaniment of E. H. Shepard's simple line drawings is abandoned in favour of tasteless and anonymous art-work drawn from the Walt Disney film.

Or consider the fate of Rudyard Kipling's *Just So Stories* in:

(312) **The Elephant's Child,** illustrated by Leonard Weisgard *Macmillan* 1970, £1·95 and:
(313) **The Beginning of the Armadilloes,** illustrated by Giuliano Maestro *Macmillan* 1970, £1·25.
The first is an exercise in flashy colour work, the second a trendy piece of pop-art, and neither is in any way justified by the nature of Kipling's text (which, incidentally, he illustrated perfectly well himself).

In few places recently however has the exploitation of 'classic' texts by picture book manufacturers been more intensive than in the re-illustration of Edward Lear. Lear, who was a professional artist as well as a 'laureate of nonsense', established in his own drawings a definitive way of looking at his songs and limericks and any adjustments that later contributors make to the balance which he has established between word and picture run the risk of distracting attention from the writing — where, especially in the longer poems, attention properly belongs.

There can really be no excuse for Dale Maxey's vulgar delineations in such a book as:

(314) **The Pobble who has no Toes** and other nonsense by Edward Lear *Collins* 1968, 95p.
or for the weak interpretations by Gerald Rose in:
(315) **The Dong with a Luminous Nose** and other poems by Edward Lear *Faber* 1969, 90p.
where the display of fizzy colour cannot hide the poverty of imagination and invention. (For purposes of quick comparison, an edition of Lear's poems may be seen at item 21, although many of the drawings are considerably reduced here, and are less well placed on the page than in the original editions).

That the work of an artist like Lear, even if 'definitive', may not be entirely sacrosanct is shown by the interpretation of those artists who have fully mastered the nuances of his wry as well as comic tone of voice. The much praised:

(316) **The Jumblies** and other nonsense verses by Edward Lear with drawings by L. Leslie Brooke *Warne* 1954, 60p.
is perhaps too insistent in its playing on farcical possibilities

(hence missing the irony and nostalgia of the poem) but the twin picture books :
(317) **The Jumblies** drawings by Edward Gorey *Chatto* 1969, 80p. (Reading, Mass. *Addison* 1968) and :
(318) **The Dong with a Luminous Nose** by Edward Lear, drawings by Edward Gorey *Chatto* 1970, 80p. (Reading, Mass. *Addison* 1969.)
are so perfect in catching every inflection of the words, and so close to the spirit of Lear's own drawings, that there can be nothing for them but praise.

12b. THE MORAL TALE

Since its earliest beginnings children's literature has been a province for adult writers with a message. Table manners, personal conduct and the state of one's soul have often seemed to be the central subjects upon which children's books should concentrate and various degrees of disapproval are registered from time to time on those books which have nothing more to offer than imaginative constructs or unwholesome levity.

Those who speak of the present time as a 'golden age' and who think of us as freed once and for all from the rationalism of Maria Edgeworth or the sermonizing of Mrs Sherwood have neglected to notice the strenuous attempts at moral teaching of one sort or another which is increasingly apparent in contemporary children's literature. The recent objections that have been lodged against such fundamentally innocent works as *Little Black Sambo*, *Billy Bunter* and the nursery rhyme 'Ten Little Nigger Boys' represent the repressive aspects of the movement, while the regular appearance of stories devised largely to aid the 'socialization' of children and adolescents represents its promotional ones. (How rarely though do any of its writers reach the incisiveness and the humanity that are among the virtues of the despised Miss Edgeworth and Mrs Sherwood).

It is therefore not surprising to find a moral school among the creators of picture books as well as among the writers of tract novels. At its simplest and most inoffensive this appears (where it has always appeared) at the level of the fable, where, fortunately for children, the moral content tends to be subordinated to the anecdote, the turning of the joke :

(319) **Aesop's Fables,** a selection illustrated by Gaynor Chapman *Hamish Hamilton* 1971, £1·25.
Each page opening is given over to a single fable, sometimes with the moral explicitly stated, sometimes with it only present in the tale (and not always clearly so, as in The Monkey and the Whale). For all the brightness of their patterning, the illustrations give no real narrative support either to the fable or its moral.

(320) **The Lion and the Rat** by Brian Wildsmith *Oxford University Press* 1963, £1·15.
In this, and several companion volumes, Brian Wildsmith devotes all his powers to developing pictorially through thirty-two pages incidents which Gaynor Chapman dealt with in two. Next to the *ABC* (15) and *123* (35) these are the books where Brian Wildsmith's talents are most successfully at work — the minimal narrative line offering many opportunities for pictorial ornamentation without endangering the point of the final pages.

(321) **The Fox and the Raven** by Ruth Hürlimann *Longman Young Books* 1972, £1·30 (Zürich *Atlantis* 1972). Another full picture-book treatment of a single fable, but less successfully managed than Brian Wildsmith's, since the expansion of the simple text seems to have been carried out in order to fill up the book rather than to add point to the tale but this may be the fault of the translator. The old moral certainly seems to have disappeared entirely.

(322) **The Mouse with the Daisy Hat** by Ruth Hürlimann *Longman Young Books* 1971, 90p. (Zürich, *Atlantis* 1971).
(323) **The Tale of Johnny Town-Mouse** by Beatrix Potter *Warne* 1918, 40p.
The greater ramifications of the fable of the town mouse and the country mouse enable Ruth Hürlimann here to follow the story more closely in her pictures, even though the text is inclined to waver between a nice conversational directness and an unnecessary amount of padding. In its extent it compares interestingly with Beatrix Potter's version (which retains and personalises the original moral). Miss Potter however is inimitable in her organisation of story and picture — despite a slight mis-connection on page 32 — and in the detail of her characterisations.

Where stories of our own invention are concerned we are not so easy-going. In examples such as 105 and 260 above, an element of didacticism has already been noted, beside which may be set such explicit statements as :

(324) **The Happy Owls** a legend illustrated by Celestino Piatti *Benn* 1965, £1·25. (Zürich, *Artemis* 1963).
where the strong, beautifully conceived paintings are betrayed by the sentimentality of the owl's sermon and their conclusive self-righteousness* ; or

(325) **The Lazy Bear** by Brian Wildsmith *Oxford University Press* 1973, £1·50.
where all the pictorial glamour that was lavished on La Fontaine is still present but where the last two pages set out the moral with uncompromising baldness ; or :

(326) **The Miracle of the Pear Tree** by György Lehoczky *Blackie* 1973, £1·45 (München, *Annette Betz*, 1971).
where the over-written text at first sentimentalises nature and then invokes God as the author of natural processes in the fashion of such traditional Sunday School fare as :

(327) **I Like** designed by Gordon Stowell *Scripture Union* 1972, 6p.

Nowhere, however, has the contemporary picture-book maker found happier hunting than in the turgid waters of 'pollution', which has undeniably become one of the great themes in present-day didacticism. Only rarely has the subject been set out with any subtlety, as in :

*Footnote : Nowhere in *The Happy Owls* is the original version of the book mentioned, prepared by Theo Van Hoytema, *Uilen-Geluk*, Amsterdam, 1895.

(328) **The Lorax** by Dr Seuss *Collins* 1972, £1·00 (NY, *Random House* 1971).
in which the Dr's customary absurdities give a more than usually informal setting to the minatory 'Unless . . .' at the end ; or :

(329) **Dinosaurs and all that Rubbish** by Michael Foreman *Hamish Hamilton* 1972, £1·40.
where the stridency of the text is off-set to some extent by the comedy of the pictures. The artist's first picture book :

(330) **The General** by Janet Charters and Michael Foreman. *Routledge* 1961, £1·25.
shows him tackling a sentimental pacifist tract with some appropriate kindergarten-style paintings, and the much later work :

(331) **Moose** by Michael Foreman. *Hamish Hamilton* 1971, £1·25.
shows how much more happily the same moral can be conveyed through under-rather than over-emphasis.

In such direct pronouncements as :

(332) **The Motormalgamation** by H. G. Fischer-Tschöp and Barbara von Johnson *Studio Vista* 1973, £1·25. (Stuttgart, 1973).
(333) **Nim and his World** by André Joanny, illustrated by Armand Laval *Macdonald* 1973, 75p. (Paris, *Editions C.P.*, 1973).
(334) **Wilkie's World** by Edith Thacher Hurd and Clement Hurd *Faber* 1973, £1·40. (NY, *Harper* 1971).
not only are there no mitigating features of textual subtlety or artistic character, but the books' own emotional standpoint seriously falsifies the ecological and human issues that are at stake. The American edition of the last was entitled 'Wilson's World'. Is there a political implication in the change of title ?

When all is said and done, none of these contemporary moralisers operates with the style and vigour of their forerunner in the field of picture books :
(335) **Struwwelpeter** merry stories and funny pictures by Heinrich Hoffman *Blackie* 1903 £1·20p, *Pan* 1972, 25p.
First published in 1845 (and in English in 1848) this is among the first children's picture books to adopt a quarto format and is in all probability the longest lived of all our original picture books. For all the obloquy that has been heaped upon its 'violence', it belongs rather to the movement towards guying the moral tradition (later refined in England by Harry Graham in *Ruthless Rhymes* and Hilaire Belloc in the *Cautionary Verses*), seeing its prime object as making children laugh. In its early forms the book was, graphically speaking, a pleasure to look at. Our present printings, and especially the paperback, are a crude travesty of the original. See the chapter on Hoffmann in B. Hürlimann *Three Centuries of Children's Books in Europe* (Bibliography item 10).

Comparisons from the Past

(336) **The English Struwwelpeter** Twentieth edition. *W. Mogg*. n.d. [c.1865].

46

(337) **The English Struwwelpeter** Thirty-eighth edition. *Griffith, Farran, Okeden & Welsh*. n.d. [c.1885].
(338) **The Little Minxes** David Bogue. n.d. [c.1855].
An early hand-coloured and early lithographed edition of the famous *Struwwelpeter*, showing the crispness of printing despite the long runs that must have been undertaken. *The Little Minxes* is just one of the very many imitations which the book engendered in Great Britain.

(339) **A Little Pretty Pocket-Book** Facsimile of the 1767 edition of one of the first books for children published by John Newbery *Oxford University Press* The Juvenile Library, 1966.
Fable and woodcut from a compendium of 'instruction and amusement', first published in 1744.

(340) **The Fables of Aesop and Others** translated into human nature. Designed and drawn on the wood by Charles H. Bennett. *W. Kent & Co.* [1857].
A book for adults using the illustrative style of a children's book.
(See also the picture fable reproduced at item 319 above).

(341) **Aesop's Fables** illustrated by Ernest Griset, *Cassell, Petter & Galpin* n.d. [1869].
A dramatic wood-engraving that contrasts well with Brian Wildsmith's *The Lion and the Rat* (320).

(342) **Pictures and Stories for Little Children** . . . *SPCK*, 1885.
A bound up series of booklets printed for sale cheaply to Sunday Schools. Each page contains a little moral tale and a wood engraved illustration.

(343) **The Little Dog Trusty** G. *Routledge & Co.* 1857. (Aunt Mavor's Picture Story Books).
One of Maria Edgeworth's less impressive moral tales dating from the beginning of the century. It has here been chopped into single syllables for 'beginning beginners'.

(344) **Little John,** or the Bright Silver Shilling. *Dean & Son.* n.d. [1852] Aunt Busy Bee's New Series of Sixpenny Books.
A lesson in the virtue of diligence.

12c. EXPERIMENTATION

In its day *Struwwelpeter* (335) was something of an experiment, and one whose success encouraged a whole range of imitations. The close dependency of picture books upon graphic techniques has automatically made them subjects for and beneficiaries of experimentation at a technical level. And, artists being what convention would have them, there has often been a good deal of playing about with the visual possibilities of the medium. Some examples have already been noted at items 37, 97, 198 and 230 and discussions of the balance between tradition and experiment are to be found in such general accounts of book illustration as those by D. Bland and R. McLean (Bibliography items 1, 2 and 13).

As with the constant reworking of traditional or classic tales, the danger of experimentation is that it is carried out for its own sake and not for any reason closely associated with the creation of a children's book as a unified work af art. The great tradition of picture books, which demands of illustrators a consciousness of the workings of narrative, is not lightly to be rejected or deemed moribund, and among the following examples of experimental work, only those which are based on a knowledge of the tradition seem likely to last.

(345) **In the Night Kitchen** by Maurice Sendak *Bodley Head* 1971, £1·25. (NY, *Harper* 1970).
A picture book at once more radical and more eclectic than *Where the Wild Things Are* (123). Maurice Sendak has taken his dreamer to a stranger land than ever Max went to and has drawn upon a wider range of graphic references (art deco, advertising, comics). For all the naturalness with which these are assimilated into Sendak's own personality as an illustrator, their very diversity indicates the book's failure to find the same kind of pointedness in the dream sequence that gave such impetus to *The Wild Things*.

(346) **Vicki** by Renate Meyer *Bodley Head* 1968, 90p.
Like *Hide and Seek* (198), a picture book without words. It was the first of Renate Meyer's picture books and presented her reviewers with serious problems of assessment. The difficulty lay not simply in the experimental nature of the graphic work – especially her adaptation of nature printing – but also in the allied novelty of her viewpoint. The book is more than anything a pictorial exploration of the intensity of child feelings, demanding not so much to be explained as to be likewise felt (a point which seems also to have passed by the writer of the dust-jacket blurb).

(347) **Momoko's Lovely Day** illustrations by Chihiro Iwasaki *Bodley Head* 1969, 85p. (Tokyo, *Shiko-Sha* 1968).
The incursion of Japanese illustrators upon world markets is a subject that awaits further discussion. Among the many now published in Europe, few have so distinctive a personal style as Chihiro Iwasaki, whose use of impressionistic water-colour washes printed on heavy gloss papers marks a new departure in technique. Impressionism, though, however beautiful, is not the most robust of illustrative styles, and Miss Iwasaki's picture books fall decidedly short where action and movement are concerned.

(348) **Story Number One** by Eugene Ionesco, illustrated by Etienne Delessert. *Harlin Quist*, distri buted in UK by *W. H. Allen* 1969, £1·25.
Whether or not the author is serious about his *Story Number One* being for children under three years of age, neither he nor his illustrator is serious about much else. As an object lesson in refined confusion the book is an impressive and highly professional compilation. But its random progress, its ill-written text and its variety of illustrative styles render it insignificant as a book for children.

(Nor is Etienne Delessert much happier with the fairly homogeneous graphic style he has adopted for :

(349) **The Tree** by Eleanor Schmid *Harlin Quist* distributed in UK by *W. H. Allen*. 1966, £1·05.
The inconsequential text is printed in a modish style that makes it almost illegible and the raw pictorial treatment of events offers little incentive to persevere).

(350) **Andromedary SR 1** by Martin Ripkens and Hans Stempel pictures by Heinz Edelmann *Michael Joseph* 1971, £1·25. (Köln, *Friedrich Middelhauve* 1970).
(351) **Ann in the Moon** by F. D. Francis, illustrated by Alan Aldridge *Purnell/Bancroft* 1970, £1·05.

Two examples of contemporary trendiness which, by pursuing novelty and humour without being aware of the mainsprings of such virtues, result in mere contrivance.

(352) **Little Blue and Little Yellow** by Leo Lionni *Brockhampton* 1962, 95p. (Holland, *Astor-Honor* 1959).
An 'abstract' picture book calling the reader to suspend any wish for a logical explanation and to react in different ways at different points of the 'story'. Visually he may be offered pictures that he will try to see 'in plan' or 'in section' but which may simply become exercises in colour mixing ; verbally he obtains an apparently realistic tale which shifts at unexpected moments into a kind of metaphor (and one which could provide Freudians with much food for thought).

(353) **Through the Window** by Charles Keeping *Oxford University Press* 1970, £1·10.

With his first picture book,
(354) **Shaun and the Carthorse** *Oxford University Press* 1966, £1·10,
Charles Keeping made dramatic use of the new possibilities in colour printing that were emerging at that time. With each successive book he sought to maximise the force of his texts through their visual presentation, experimenting not merely in kaleidoscopic colour variations but also in colour symbolism :
(355) **Charlie, Charlotte and the Golden Canary** *Oxford University Press* 1967, £1·00
and the dramatic use of page sequences and of double page spreads :
(356) **Joseph's Yard** *Oxford University Press* 1969, £1·00.
Through the Window more than any previous book justified this experimental approach, bringing together the elements noted above to give energy and depth to an apparently simple sequence of events. Unlike many *soi-disant* revolutionaries in the world of picture books, Keeping has recognised the interdependence of word and image, acknowledging through every one of his own picture books the *narrative* force of the illustrations. It is a strength noted earlier too in his version of *The Christmas Story* (245).

(357) **King Tree** by Fiona French. *Oxford University Press* 1973, £1·50.
Present culmination of an experimental manner that explores not new styles or processes but old forms. In previous books :
(358) **Jack of Hearts** by Fiona French *Oxford University Press* 1970, £1·25.
(359) **Huni** by Fiona French *Oxford University Press* 1971, £1·25.
(360) **The Blue Bird** by Fiona French *Oxford University Press* 1972 £1·25.
Fiona French created stories to fit the illustrative possibilities of playing card design, ancient Egyptian painting and Chinese ceramic art. Each impressed by the cleverness of the idea and the skill of its execution rather than by its

success as an integrated picture-story. With *King Tree*, however, the shape and the telling of the tale harmonise perfectly with the poise and the baroque fantasy of the adopted decorative style.

Comparisons from the Past

Experimentation is always to be found (indeed much of the Victorian era tended towards the experimental in its approach to children's books) but a few examples here have been given of notable European books from the turn of the century and the nineteen twenties and thirties when new graphic techniques gave a special impetus to children's book production :

(361) **La Civilité Puérile et Honnete** expliquée par l'oncle Eugène et illustrée par M.B. de Monvel. Paris, *E. Plon* n.d. [c.1885]
A witty commentary on child manners by one of the master craftsmen of book illustration, noted especially for his brilliantly inventive handling of colour and page design.

(362) **Fitzebutze** von Paula & Richard Dehmel, mit Bildern von Ernst Kreidolf. Leipzig. 1968.
A facsimile reprint of the Insel Verlag edition of 1900.

(363) **Skazki**

(364) **Volga** Boghatyr Volga translated by F. Taborsky, illustrated by I. Ya. Bilibin. V Praze [1904 ?] Builini Series.
Two examples of the highly individual use of half-tone colour printing that occurred in Russia at the turn of the century.

(365) **Voyages et Glorieuses Découvertes des Grands Navigateurs et Explorateurs Français** Illustré par Edy Legrand. Paris, *Tolmer*, 1921.
Colour application by stencil in a luxurious example of French book design.

(366) **Fables de La Fontaine** Avec Images de André Hellé. *Nancy, Berger-Levrault.* n.d. [?1930].

(367) **Daniel Boone** (cover title) edited by Esther Averill and Lila Stanley. Lithographs in colour by Fedor Rojankovsky. *Faber*, 1931.

(368) **George Washington** by Ingri and Edgar Parin d'Aulaire. Garden City, *Doubleday*, 1936.
'Lithographed on stone in five colours by the authors and printed by offset lithography . . .'

(369) **Repka** illustrated by Yu. Vasnetsov, Moscow 1936.
A twin of the turnip story (293), and a further example of the use of offset lithography by Russian printers in the 1930's. (See item 253 above).

(370) **L'Ane et le Cheval** par Marcel Aymé. Images de M. Parry. *Librairie Gallimard*, 1937. Un Conte du Chat Perché.
A French children's story using an illustrative style comparable to, and perhaps influenced by the Russian examples of the period.

(371) **This Year Next Year** by Walter de la Mare. Illustrated by Harold Jones. *Faber*, 1937.
A small masterpiece of English book design and colour printing from the nineteen thirties.

13. AUDIO-VIZ

One area of experimentation not open to the Victorian makers of picture books is that created by electronics. The arrival of cheap electrical gadgets of all kinds in the child's world has stimulated much thought about their adaptation to educational processes and it is not surprising to find picture books, with their strong visual emphasis, lending themselves to exploitation.

At the simplest level this has resulted in a number of highly praised picture books being converted into film-strips, primarily to enable their stories to be told to a large group of children without the book having to be held up to view and without the danger that many children would not see the pictures anyway. A second advantage, it is claimed, is that the film-strip brings the picture book into the charmed circle of mechanical entertainment, offering as well as its own pictures (a) the opportunity to operate a machine, and (b) an experience corresponding in some ways to the viewing of colour television.

It is quite possible that social and educational arguments of this kind, supporting the conversion of picture books into film-strips, are at their own level excellent. There is a danger, however, that in welcoming the conversion we may lose sight of the true nature of the picture book itself. For, in general, it is not a social or an educational instrument, but a cultural one and it is, at its best, designed less for public functions than for the intimate colloquy of author and artist to reader (whether that reader be a child or an adult sitting with a child). By interrupting this relationship, by placing equipment between the book and its recipient, by editing and altering the original design of picture books, the film-strip may in fact be converting a spontaneous and natural form of communication into a forced and unnatural one (or, in MacLuhanite terms, the hot medium gets decidedly cooler). This is especially obvious in the case of a book like :

(372) **The Tale of Peter Rabbit** (Weston Woods Filmstrip no. FS 33)
where the size of the book and the tone of the author's voice demand an enclosed, comfortable one-to-one relationship between book and reader – to say nothing of the fact that the colours of the film-strip are even more washed out than the printed colours of current editions of the book. With :

(373) **Millions of Cats** (Weston Woods Filmstrip no. FS 5) a different form of interference occurs because the rigid limitation of the film-strip's frame cannot cope with Wanda Gág's flexible use of pages – in fact only rarely does any book which makes creative use of double-page spreads lend itself successfully to film-strip conversion. (In this case too, the essential element of Wanda Gág's *written* text is omitted – as are also, for instance, the entertaining conversation bubbles in Edward Ardizzone's *Little Tim*):

Item 272

Framed illustrations (1). Frames contributing to a picture's total effect: a boy leans out to collect an apple; a rabbit hops over the bottom while the snail is beginning his journey along the top (continued in later pictures); a woodwork frame becomes almost part of the architecture.

Item 19

Item 25

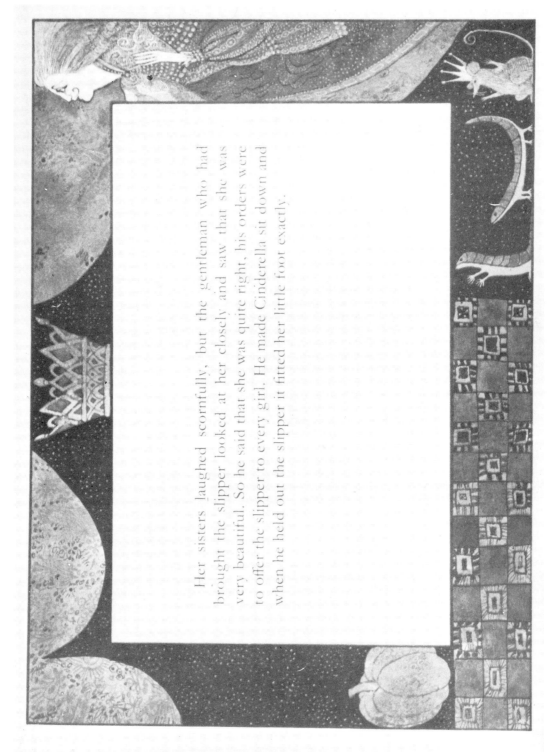

Her sisters laughed scornfully, but the gentleman who had brought the slipper looked at her closely and saw that she was very beautiful. So he said that she was quite right, his orders were to offer the slipper to every girl. He made Cinderella sit down and when he held out the slipper it fitted her little foot exactly.

Item 215   **Framed illustrations (2).** Offstage, Cinderella's prince, accompanied by rat, lizards and pumpkin, look across the text towards the slipper-fitting scene.

One day Bartek set off up a steep path
through the trees that led to one of these
ponds. The sun blazed down, and Bartek
strode along whistling. As he passed a
patch of bushes he heard a faint echo of
the tune he was whistling, and stopped
to listen.

A voice came gently to his ears:
"Help me, Bartek, please help me!"
He looked up and down the road but
there was nobody to be seen.

The whisper came again, fainter than
before. "Help me, Bartek! Look under
the wild rose."

Bartek pushed branches and creepers
apart and saw, caught among the thorny
stems of the dog-rose bush, a large

green frog. Its skin was withered and
dry, and it was panting for breath.

"Help me, Bartek, please!" it gasped.
"Carry me to the pond in your sieve.
I need water badly. I've been trapped
in the thorns for so long that if I am
left like this much longer I shall die.
I am the King of the Frogs, and I shall
repay you richly one day for your
kindness."

"Of course I shall help you," said
Bartek, "and I don't expect anything
in return."

He put a layer of leaves and moss in
the bottom of the sieve, pulled the stems
of the rose bush aside and freed the Frog
King from their thorns.

Item 232

Item 267 **Framed illustrations (3).** Bartek's journey along the path and past the frog takes place
across the text that describes it (above); while below, the decorated frame adds to and
comments on the double page of pictures and text.

Item 280

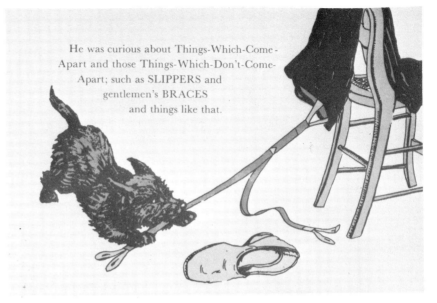

He was curious about Things-Which-Come-
Apart and those Things-Which-Don't-Come-
Apart; such as SLIPPERS and
gentlemen's BRACES
and things like that.

Item 107

Item 109

He saw a boy playing with his dog. Whenever
the boy whistled, the dog ran straight to him.

Peter tried and tried to whistle, but he couldn't.
So instead he began to turn himself around—
around and around he whirled . . .
faster and faster . . . .

From reality to abstraction. A sequence of examples which show different illustrative styles
in sequence from Beatrix Potter's portrait of Farmer Potatoes, which is said to have been done
from a photograph, to Leo Lionni's adventure in abstraction *Little Blue and Little Yellow.*

across the yard

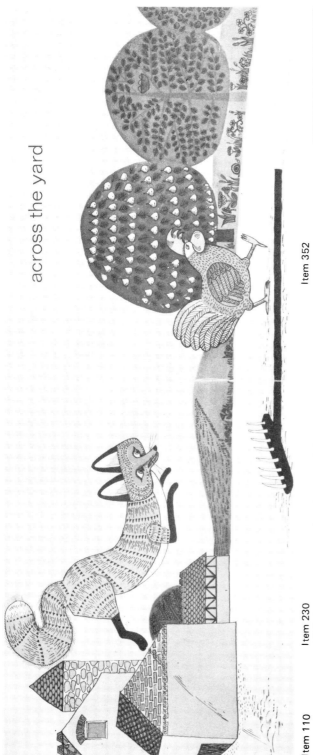

Item 110

Now Cushion ran to help father.

Item 230

But little blue went out to look for little yellow.

Item 352

Item 351

Item 346

Item 356

Item 348

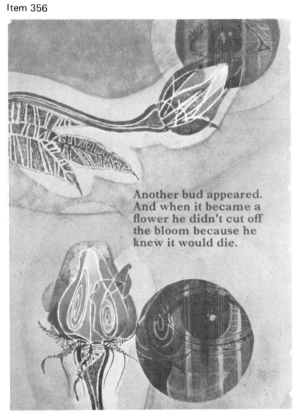

Another bud appeared.
And when it became a
flower he didn't cut off
the bloom because he
knew it would die.

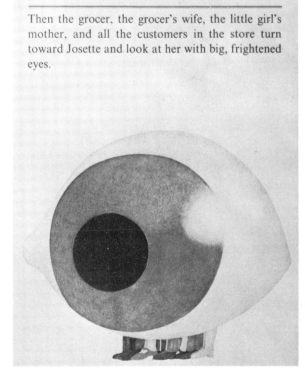

Then the grocer, the grocer's wife, the little girl's mother, and all the customers in the store turn toward Josette and look at her with big, frightened eyes.

Experiment. Four illustrations consciously aiming at a new visual style; at least three of them also call upon fairly sophisticated graphic methods in their original production.

AND FELL THROUGH THE DARK, OUT OF HIS CLOTHES

↑ Item 345   ↓ Item 266

"That will keep the cow from falling off the roof." And he began to whistle as he went on with his work.

Pastiche. The conscious echoing of styles of the past: Wanda Gag and the chapbook woodcuts, Fiona French and Egyptian painting, Margot Zemach and the English colour print, Maurice Sendak and art deco.

Item 359

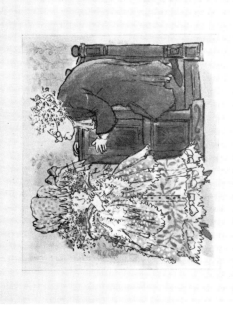

Item 128

Long ago, Egypt was ruled by a mighty Pharaoh. He was a wise man and his reign was long and peaceful. When he grew old he knew that the time had come to find out whether his son, Humi, would be strong enough to rule Egypt after him. So he sent him on a journey.

"Go down to the banks of the River Nile," he said. "And follow the great Sun god, Ra, on his way through the night hours. If you reach the daylight again you will be strong enough to wear the crown of Egypt." Humi went down to the river, and there he saw a strange man standing in a boat.

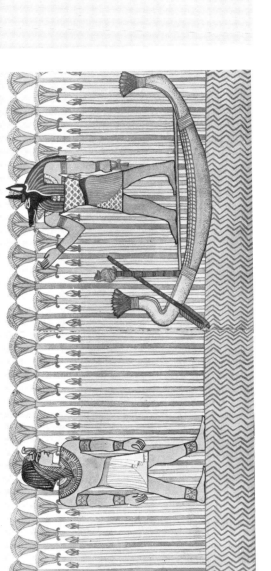

Item 269

Item 87

Randolph Caldecott and Maurice Sendak.
A small acknowledgement to the presiding
geniuses of this exhibition, their agreement
on the essential principles of illustration
and, nonetheless, their assertion of a
completely individual personality.

(374) **Little Tim and the Brave Sea Captain** (Weston Woods Filmstrip no. FS 47)
does however show some of the positive features of film-strip as a way of presenting picture books to children. Quite apart from the fact that many of the monochrome drawings in the book are now coloured in – with only one or two noticeably out of harmony with the original coloured illustrations – the sequence of pictures stands more strongly on its own than in the film-strips noted above. This is partly because of the strong narrative content of Ardizzone's drawing and partly because the story is far less a literary work in its own right.

Another approach ideally suited to film-strip presentation is :

(375) **What Do You Say, Dear ?** by Sesyle Joslin, pictures by Maurice Sendak (Weston Woods Filmstrip FS 49)
where the question-and-answer sequence fits perfectly into frame-by-frame movement (and where the reduction and elongation necessary to accommodate the double-page answers contrasts well with the squarer question pages).

Not content with editing picture books into film-strip form (which, be it said, is often done with care and intelligence) the manufacturers have also taken the process further and have added synchronised, taped or recorded sound-tracks, or have abandoned the static frame-by-frame progress in favour of creating a totally animated sound film.

Even at the first of these stages one is leaving behind the world of picture books and entering a territory where new criteria are required for judgement. The singing of :

(376) **The Fox Went Out on a Chilly Night** (Weston Woods Filmstrip and Cassette SF 58),
for instance, reduces the picture element almost to nothing ; and the voice and music of :

(377) **Where the Wild Things Are** (Weston Woods Filmstrip and Cassette SF 84C)
turns a private book into a public entertainment – jazz accompaniment and all.

With such animated films as :
(378) **Drummer Hoff**
and :
(379) **Rosie's Walk**

opportunities are available to the director beyond those open to the conventional picture-book artist and the notable success of these works, while owing a deep debt to the originators, must be measured within the traditions of the cartoon film.

Selective Bibliography

The length of the following book-list should not in any way be equated with strength. Very little serious criticism of children's book illustration has been published and the works noted here will be chiefly useful in filling out a descriptive background to the present catalogue, or in directing attention to statements on their work by the illustrators themselves. A number of articles from journals have been included – those by myself not in any spirit of self-aggrandisement but merely to supplement critical points made above. Many other books and articles, chiefly American, have been intentionally omitted since, like so much that passes for criticism of children's books in the United States of America, they are exercises only in the tattling or the sycophantic.

I : General and historical studies

1
Bland, David **The history of book illustration ;** the illuminated manuscript and the printed book. Second edition, London. *Faber & Faber*, 1969. First published 1958.
Our most authoritative history whose scale however often confines the author to a very limited discussion of movements in children's book illustration and the work of individual illustrators.

2
Bland, David **The illustration of books.** Third edition, London, *Faber & Faber* 1962. First published 1951.
A brief history of the subject – later to be expanded as the above item, but unlike that volume treating children's books in a separate chapter. The Second Part on 'Processes and their application' provides a useful summary of technical aspects, while the Introduction touches upon several issues central to the task of criticizing illustrated books.

3
Crouch, Marcus **Treasure seekers and borrowers ;** children's books in Britain 1900–1960. London, *The Library Association*, 1962.
Sketches in the background to contemporary picture-book production.

4
Darton, F. J. Harvey **Children's books in England ;** five centuries of social life. Second edition, *Cambridge University Press* 1958. First published 1932.
A major historical discussion rich in detailed knowledge and insight. Consideration of picture books, however, tends to be subordinated to the fuller discussion of literary and publishing fashions.

5
Egoff, Sheila ; G. T. Stubbs and L. F. Ashley **Only connect ;** readings on children's literature. Toronto, *Oxford University Press*, 1969.
A 'reader' ; the essays forming its contents are drawn from many sources and cover many aspects of children's books.

6
Eyre, Frank **British children's books in the twentieth century,** London, *Longman*, 1971.
Based on a British Council Pamphlet '20th Century Children's Books', 1952.
Chapter two discusses 'Books with Pictures'.

7
Hardie, Martin **English coloured books,** with an introduction by James Laver. Reprinted. Bath, *Kingsmead Reprints*, 1973, First published 1906.
Chapter twenty-two deals with the work of Edmund Evans, apart from which, children's books receive only cursory treatment.

8
Haviland, Virginia ed. **Children's literature ;** views and reviews. Glenview, Ill. *Scott, Foresman*, 1973.
A 'reader' which owes more than its form to the previously published *Only connect* (item 5 above).

9
Hürlimann, Bettina **Picture-book world.** Translated and edited by Brian W. Alderson . . . with a bio-bibliographical supplement by Elisabeth Waldmann. London, *Oxford University Press*, 1968. First published as Die Welt im Bilderbuch, Zürich, 1965.
A rather superficial survey, country by country, accompanied by many illustrations and rounded off with notes and book-lists of more than one hundred and fifty modern illustrators. The references appended to these notes and contained in the section 'Further reading' can supplement this present list.

10
Hürlimann, Bettina **Three centuries of children's books in Europe.** Translated and edited by Brian W. Alderson. London, *Oxford University Press*, 1967. First published as : Europäische Kinderbücher in drei Jahrhunderten. Zürich 1959. The English translation is of the second edition, Zürich, 1963.
A general discussion of various aspects of the development of children's literature in Europe, edited with English readers in mind. Chapter four is an account of 'Struwwelpeter' Hoffmann, chapter fifteen of Jean de Brunhoff. It is followed by a survey chapter that was later expanded into item 9 above.

11
Künnemann, Horst **Profile Zeitgenossischer Bilderbuchmacher** Weinheim, *Beltz Verlag*, 1972.
A series of illustrated essays including discussions of the work of John Burningham, Walt Disney, Maurice Sendak, Dr. Seuss and Brian Wildsmith.

12
MacCann, Donnarae & Olga Richard **The Child's First Books ;** a critical study of pictures and texts. NY, *H. W. Wilson*, 1973.
An attempt to grapple with principles, but prevented from being either 'critical' or 'a study' by its naiveté and its ill-defined criteria.

13
McLean, Ruari **Victorian book design and colour printing.** Second edition, London. *Faber & Faber*, 1972. First published 1963 and now enlarged to a more impressive but less easily usable format. The text offers much out-of-the-way information about the printing of Victorian children's books (accompanied by many illustrations), but lacks a firm critical attitude in assessing them.

14
Mahony, Bertha E. ; Louise Payson Latimer and Beulah Folmsbee eds. **Illustrators of children's books 1744–1945** Boston, *The Horn Book Inc.* 1947.
A collection of essays and bibliographies which form the most substantial introduction to the subject so far published. Bibliographical and critical weakness,

excusable in a pioneer work of this kind, are unfortunately more marked in its two successor volumes:
Viguers, Ruth Hill; Marcia Dalphin and Bertha Mahony Miller eds. **Illustrators of children's books 1946–1956.** Boston, *The Horn Book*, 1958.
and:
Kingman, Lee; Joanna Foster and Ruth Giles Lontoft eds. **Illustrators of children's books 1957–1966,** Boston, *The Horn Book*, 1968.

15
Morris, Charles H. **The illustration of children's books.** London, *The Library Association*, 1957 (LA Pamphlets No. 16). A swift historical survey which owes much to sources noted elsewhere in this bibliography.

16
Muir, Percy **English children's books 1600–1900.** London, *Batsford*, 1954.
Chapter seven discusses picture books and chapter eight stands as one of the only attempts to categorise and describe 'nick nacks'.

17
Muir, Percy **Victorian illustrated books.** London, *Batsford*, 1971.
A disorganized and unreliable volume, which nonetheless contains a wealth of information and anecdote.

18
St John, Judith ed. **The Osborne collection of early children's books 1566–1910**; a catalogue. *Toronto Public Library,* 1958.
Not merely a catalogue but an invaluable (and handsomely printed) reference book.

19
Sketchley, R. E. D. **English book illustration of today**; appreciations of the work of living English illustrators with lists of their books. With an introduction by Alfred W. Pollard. London, *Kegan Paul, Trench, Trubner & Co.* 1903.
Chapter four discusses 'Some children's books illustrators' and accompanying bibliographies are provided.

20
Smith, Janet Adam **Children's illustrated books.** London, *Collins*, 1948 (Britain in Pictures).
For all its brevity this is one of the most positive and readable commentaries on its subject, striking a fine balance in its discussion of the illustrator's methods and his responsibility towards his text.

21
Smith, Lillian. H. **The unreluctant years**; a critical approach to children's literature. Chicago, *American Library Association*, 1953.
Chapter eight on 'Picture Books' represents one of the few sustained attempts to reconcile the critical response of adults to picture books with the instinctive response of children.

22
Thwaite, M. F. **From primer to pleasure in reading**; an introduction to the history of children's books in England . . . second edition. London, *The Library Association*, 1972. First published 1963.
Chapter VIII sketches in some of the main events in picture-book making during the nineteenth and early twentieth centuries.

23
White, Dorothy Neal **Books before five.** *Oxford University Press* for the New Zealand Council for Educational Research, 1954.
A unique study of one child's reactions to picture books, as observed by her mother who was also a distinguished children's librarian.

II: **Books and articles on specific topics or illustrators**
ABC's
24
McLean, Ruari **Pictorial Alphabets.** London, *Studio Vista*, 1969.
A brief and unhelpful picture book.

25
Garrett, Pat. **ABC's from A to Z**. *Children's Book Review* Occasional List No. 1 April 1971.
A note on the genre, followed by reviews.

Ardizzone
26
Alderson, Brian **Edward Ardizzone**; a preliminary hand-list of his illustrated books 1929–1970, in *The Private Library*, quarterly journal of the Private Libraries Association, Second series Vol. 5 No. 1 Spring 1972. Issued simultaneously as a paper bound offprint.
An attempt to described in detail (with a few brief comments) the books of a single illustrator. Page 4 contains a list of references of which the following shed fuller biographical or critical light on the subject:—

27
Ardizzone, Edward **The born illustrator,** in *Motif* No. 1 November, 1958. Reprinted in Signal No. 3 September, 1970.

28
Ardizzone, Edward **Creation of a picture book,** in *Top of the News*. December 1959. Reprinted in *Only Connect*, ed. S. Egoff et al. (item 5 above).

29
Ardizzone, Edward **The young Ardizzone**; an autobiographical fragment. London, *Studio Vista*, 1970.

30
Tucker, Nicholas **Edward Ardizzone**, in *Children's Literature in Education* No. 3, November, 1970.

Brooke
31
Moore, Anne Carroll, **L, Leslie Brooke** in *Horn Book Magazine*, May 1941 (an issue devoted entirely to Leslie Brooke). This and another article by A. C. Moore and Lillian H. Smith's 'Canadian Tribute' are reprinted in 'A Horn Book Sampler', edited by Norma R. Fryatt, Boston, *The Horn Book*, 1959.

Brunhoff
32
Leach, Edmund **Babar's civilisation analysed,** in *New Society* 20 December 1962. Reprinted in item 5.

Caldecott
33
Blackburn, Henry **Randolph Caldecott**; a personal memoir of his early art career. London, *Sampson Low* n.d.

34
Laws, Frederick **Randolph Caldecott** in *The Saturday Book* No. 16 London, *Hutchinson* n.d. (1956) Reprinted in item 5.

Disney

35

Sayers, Frances Clarke **Walt Disney accused,** in *Horn Book Magazine*, December 1965. Reprinted in item 8.

Doyle

36

Hambourg, Daria **Richard Doyle;** his life and work. London, *Art and Technics* 1948.

Evans

37

McLean, Ruari ed. **The reminiscences of Edmund Evans.** Oxford, *Clarendon Press*, 1967.
An autobiographical essay by the leading Victorian engraver and printer of children's picture books. The editor provides a long Introduction and a chronological 'selective list' of Evans's colour printing.

Fairy Tales

38

Alderson, Brian W. **Calliope rolled flat,** in *Children's Book News* Vol. 3 No. 5. September, 1968 (Broadsides 1).
An assertion of the claims of fairy-tale texts.

Gág

39

Evans, Ernestine **Wanda Gag as a writer,** in *Horn Book Magazine*, May, 1947. Reprinted in 'A Horn Book Sampler'. (o.p. cit. 31 above).

Greenaway

40

Spielmann, M. H. and G. S. Layard **Kate Greenaway.** London, *Adam & Charles Black*, 1905.
The standard biography.

Keeping

41

Keeping, Charles **Illustration in children's books,** in *Children's Literature in Education* No. 1 March, 1970.
The foremost of a number of articles where Charles Keeping has set out his views on book illustration.

Lear

42

Davidson, Angus **Edward Lear,** landscape painter and nonsense poet (1812–1888) London, *John Murray*, 1938. Reprinted with a new preface, 1968.

43

Noakes, Vivien **Edward Lear;** the life of a wanderer. London, *Collins*, 1968.

44

Fisher, Crispin **A load of nonsense;** Edward Lear resurrected by four publishers, in *Growing Point* Vol. 8 No. 5. November, 1969. Reprinted in item 8.

45

Alderson, Brian **Non-sense and sensibility,** in *Children's Book News* Vol. 5 No. 1, January, 1970.

Nursery Rhymes

46

Opie, Iona and Peter **The Oxford Dictionary of Nursery Rhymes.** Oxford, *Clarendon Press*, 1951.

47

Sendak, Maurice **Mother Goose's garnishings,** in *Book Week* 31 October 1965. Reprinted in item 8.
A critique of the illustration of nursery rhymes which says much about the author's own values in book illustration.

48

Opie, Iona and Peter **Three centuries of nursery rhymes and poetry for children.** London, *National Book League*, 1973.
An exhibition catalogue of great bibliographical value.

123's

49

Garrett, Pat **Counting books,** *Children's Book Review*. Occasional List No. 2 October, 1971.
A companion to item 25 above.

Peake

50

Peake, Mervyn **The craft of the lead pencil.** London, *Allan Wingate*, n.d. [1946].

51

Peake, Mervyn **The drawings of Mervyn Peake.** London, *Grey Walls Press*, 1949. The Artist's Preface has been reprinted in Signal No. 1, January 1970.
This and the former essay, although primarily on drawing, represent a classic statement on the responsibility of artists and illustrators alike.

52

Gilmore, Maeve **A world away;** a memoir of Mervyn Peake. London, *Gollancz*, 1970.

53

National Book League **Word and Image III. Mervyn Peake 1911–1968.** London, *NBL* 1972.
Catalogue of an exhibition, which includes further references to the artist's illustrative work.

Pop-Ups

54

Chambers, Aidan **A peep at the pop-ups,** in *Children's Book News* Vol. 5 No. 2, March, 1970 (Broadsides).

Potter

55

Lane, Margaret **The Tale of Beatrix Potter;** a biography. Revised edition, London, *Frederick Warne & Co.* 1968. First published 1946.

56

The Art of Beatrix Potter with an appreciation by Anne Carroll Moore and notes to each section by Enid and Leslie Linder. Revised edition, London, *Frederick Warne,* 1972. First published 1955.

57

Linder, Leslie **A History of the Writings of Beatrix Potter,** including unpublished work. London, *Frederick Warne*, 1971.
A systematic documentary account, heavily illustrated and containing a series of useful bibliographical appendices.

Sendak

58

Hentoff, Nat **Among the Wild Things,** in *The New Yorker*, 22 January 1966. Reprinted in item 5.
A discussion of Maurice Sendak's work up to 1966, which includes several long excerpts from interviews with the artist.

59

Sendak, Maurice [Introduction to] *Pictures by* Maurice Sendak (Catalogue item 124).
A concise and direct acknowledgement by the artist of influences from the past by whom he is 'happily haunted'. Most of the picture books mentioned are included in the exhibition. (See also item 47 above).

Trends

60
Alderson, Brian **Impenetrable designs,** in *Children's Book News,* Volume 5 No. 3, May, 1970.
On the over-elaboration of art-work in picture books.

61
Hogarth, Grace **Illustration ?** in *Children's Book News*
Vol. 5 No. 1, January, 1970 ; to which a reply was published
in the subsequent issue (March, 1970) :

62
Illustration : another approach, by Charles Keeping.

Index

INDEX OF AUTHORS AND ILLUSTRATORS